A
COLANDER,
CAKE STAND,
AND *My Grandfather's*
IRON SKILLET

A
COLANDER,
CAKE STAND,
AND *My Grandfather's*
IRON SKILLET

Today's Top Chefs *on the* Stories *and* Recipes
Behind Their Most Treasured Kitchen Tools

Edited by
ERIN BYERS MURRAY

SPRING HOUSE PRESS

Publisher: Paul McGahren
Editorial Director: Matthew Teague
Editor: Erin Byers Murray
Copy Editor: Li Agen
Design: Lindsay Hess
Photography: Danielle Atkins
Illustration: Andrew Vastagh

Spring House Press
3613 Brush Hill Court
Nashville, TN 37216

ISBN: 978-1-940611-36-5
Library of Congress Control Number: 2016933083
Printed in China
First Printing: July 2016

Note: The following list contains names used in *A Colander, Cake Stand &
My Grandfather's Iron Skillet* that may be registered with the United States
Copyright Office:
Callebaut, Chasseur, Contadina, Cuisinart, Dexter-Russell, Duke's, El Rey,
F.Dick, Ghirardelli, Grillworks, Kentucky Legend, Kershaw, KitchenAid, La
Quercia, Lee Kum Kee, Lindt, Microplane, Pastene, Revere Ware, Shun Knives,
Tenure Ceramics, Valrhona, White Lily, Williams-Sonoma

To learn more about Spring House Press books, or to find
a retailer near you, email info@springhousepress.com
or visit us at www.springhousepress.com.

THANKS

There are a lot of people who helped make this book happen—I owe them a tremendous amount of gratitude (and probably a drink or two). First and foremost, the credit for this project goes to the chefs themselves—my sincere thanks to each of them for taking the time to think, reflect, write, and contribute when they were also juggling so many other tasks and projects. To that end, it would be impossible to have pulled this off without the many, many chefs' assistants, publicists, handlers, and gatekeepers who work with these professionals, many of whom help them navigate what I can only imagine is a barrage of requests just like this one. Thank you for opening the door to this idea, answering my many emails, gathering the materials, and generally being a wonderful group of people to work with.

Thank you to Matthew Teague and Paul McGahren of Spring House Press who were both so encouraging and easy to work with—I appreciate them letting me explore such a meaningful topic. Our designer, Lindsay Hess, put all of the right visual pieces in place for the project, while Danielle Atkins, a rock star photographer, completely nailed the images—she is a huge asset both for what she can see through her lens as well as her keen organizational skills. Thanks, too, to the Food Sheriff, Jesse Goldstein, who very kindly allowed us the use of his East Nashville office and studio space for the photo shoot (complete with happy hour)—the fully loaded kitchen has been outfitted by KitchenAid, making it my new favorite place to work and play. We also had some assists from chefs Rebekah Turshen and Dale Levitski, as well as the folks at Porter Road Butcher, Rolf & Daughters, and food stylist Teresa Blackburn, who all pitched in with items large and small to make the photos come together. A special shout out goes to Shannon Reed of Coastal Custom Knifeworks, who provided us with one of his stunning oyster knives, as well as John Donovan, whose new line of tableware, Tenure Ceramics, made it onto more than few of these pages.

Lastly, I'm so grateful and lucky to have such a supportive family. Thanks especially to Dave, Charlie, and Maggie for your patience, laughter, and wealth of good hugs.

CONTENTS

8   *Foreword by J. Kenji López-Alt*

10   *Introduction*

14   Conical Steamer | *Andrew Zimmern*

20   An Old Colander | *Jeremy Sewall*

24   Knife Block | *Jonathan Benno*

29   Switchblade & Pocketknife | *Jonathon Sawyer*

34   Copper-Bottom Revere Ware Pots | *Sarah Schafer*

38   Baker's Spatula | *Kyle Mendenhall*

42   Chasseur Sauté Pan | *Robert Wiedmaier*

46   Cast Iron Pan and Silver Spoon | *Rob Newton*

50   Biscuit Cutter | *Tandy Wilson*

54   Copper Jam Pot | *Nicole Krasinski*

58   Boning Knife | *Chris Shepherd*

62   Antique Cleaver | *Steven Satterfield*

67   Metal Skewer | *Stuart Brioza*

72   Meme's Cast Iron Skillet | *Virginia Willis*

76   Universal Meat Grinder | *Norman Van Aken*

80   Balloon Whisk | *Dale Levitski*

84   Plating Spoon | *Zachary Espinosa*

88   Oyster Knife | *Steve McHugh*

92   Wood-Burning Indoor Grill | *Fry Ford*

96 Wooden Spoon | *Kevin Gillespie*

100 Rolling Pin | *Natalie Chanin*

104 Sharkskin Wasabi Grater | *Ken Oringer*

107 Grandfather's Skillet | *Linton Hopkins*

110 Mortar and Pestle | *Alon Shaya*

114 Coconut Bench Scraper | *Bruce Sherman*

118 Fluted Parisian Scoops | *Timothy Hollingsworth*

122 Mini Meat Fork | *Slade Rushing*

126 Hand-Crank Cheese Grater | *Michael Scelfo*

131 Wooden Spoon | *David Guas*

136 Microplane | *Sean Brasel*

140 Copper Bowl | *Anne Willan*

145 Cake Stand | *Rebekah Turshen*

151 Double Boiler | *Chris Kimball*

156 Tarte Tatin Pan | *Seth Raynor*

162 Collection of Wooden Spoons | *Margot McCormack*

166 Depression-Glass Juicer | *Jody Adams*

171 KitchenAid Stand Mixer | *Joanne Chang*

177 *Index*

179 *Recipe Index*

181 *Contributors*

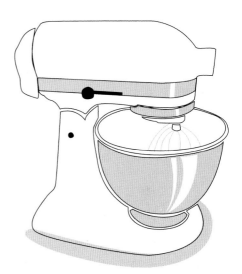

FOREWORD

I'm a kitchen gear junkie, but it's the simple tools I grew with as a cook that I treasure most. The carbon steel knife I found at a New York flea market. The Japanese *suribachi* that I inherited from my mother. The olive-wood spoon I bought while tasting wine and getting lost with my wife in Burgundy.

Line cooks are not known for their emotional fragility, but I'll never forget that Saturday night shift where I heard a brief cry of despair followed by a low moan of anguish. The battle-scarred wooden spoon my colleague had been using for nearly two decades, with its corners worn down to fit the corners of a pot just so, its color faded by stains from a thousand sauces, its handle molded by time and use to fit his

> *Cooks are rightfully attached to their tools.*
> *They are more than a simple means to an end.*
> *They are the partners and secret puppet masters*
> *of the kitchen, subtly affecting every dish you*
> *cook, weighing in on every menu decision.*

hand perfectly, had finally given in and snapped mid-stir inside a pot of risotto.

Cooks are rightfully attached to their tools. They are more than a simple means to an end. They are the partners and secret puppet masters of the kitchen, subtly affecting every dish you cook, weighing in on every menu decision you make. Likewise, seeing the tools that people use to cook with and hearing their stories can give you invaluable insight into their thought process and clues as to what their food will taste like, perhaps even more so than peering into their fridge.

Of course, this means that chef's food can never be exactly replicated. But that's OK: Making them with *your* hands and *your* tools makes them *your* food.

J. Kenji López-Alt

Author of *The Food Lab: Better Home Cooking Through Science* and managing culinary director of SeriousEats.com.

INTRODUCTION

There are three drawers in my kitchen that hold most of my "odds and ends" kitchen tools. A Microplane, some pastry brushes, a melon baller, an oyster knife. On the counter, there's a knife block and a couple of containers, each overstuffed with spatulas, wooden spoons, whisks, and ladles. Like most people, I have a few go-to favorites, the tools I grab without thinking. A specific wooden spoon with an almost sharpened edge that is great for breaking up sausage as it browns. The squat little paring knife that I pull out to cut up apples for my son.

Until I started down the path of collecting stories for this project, I hadn't considered which of the items that fill my kitchen space might be my favorite—it's like picking a favorite child, right? They're all precious, perfect, and imperfect in their own way. But as the months of collecting stories slid by, I found myself whittling down the list a bit. That plastic-handled oyster knife is something I only pull out a few times a year. It reminds me of the days I spent working on an oyster farm, especially when I get to stand on my deck, shucking oysters for my family and friends. There is what I call the "egg pan" which is a small, six-inch skillet that I pull out every single morning—it's the perfect size for quickly scrambling up a small pile of eggs for our four-person family before the day gets crazy. (Or, usually, while it's getting there.)

But if I had to choose just one (as the chefs included in this book have done), I would go with my flame-colored Le Creuset Dutch oven. It was a wedding gift chosen from our registry, one of those gifts that I picked out because I knew it would last a lifetime and stand up to just about anything. And so far it has. Ten years into our marriage, it's held up through countless marathon cooking sessions and a couple of moves. It's seen everything from soup and pasta sauce to roasts and bread. It's acted as a necessary distraction for both of my kids who, at various ages, have camped out on the floor knocking a couple of wooden spoons around its enameled sides while I wrapped up dinner. It's just heavy enough to be awkward, especially when I need to pour something out of it, like my favorite chili recipe, which starts in that pot before simmering for hours in a slow cooker. There are dings and nicks

It was brand new and oh-so-shiny. It signaled a new beginning of a life of coupledom, of a life cooking for and with another person. It signaled what I hoped would be a partnership grounded in the kitchen.

along its sides and it looks like someone took a bite out of the black button handle on the lid. (I've dropped the lid a few times, which has done plenty of damage to my floors, too.)

The pot wasn't passed down from a family member or a discovery made in a flea market. It was brand new and oh-so-shiny when I first opened the box. To me, it signaled a new beginning of a life of coupledom, of a life cooking for and with another person. It signaled what I hoped would be a partnership grounded in the kitchen. Ten years later, I can tell you that it's provided all of that and so much more. I can't remember the first thing I made in that pot, but I can tell you that just about everything that's come out of it since—even the recipe fails—has been made with love.

Whether it's a Le Creuset Dutch oven, an old colander, a recovered cake stand, or a wooden spoon, kitchen tools carry our stories. For this project, I asked thirty-seven chefs to choose their favorite tool, the one they turn to again and again or the one that offers a look into their cooking philosophy, and tell us what makes it so special.

What I learned is that for most chefs, a beloved—and many times overworked—tool can offer insight into how they became the cook they are today. A spoon uncovered in a Goodwill store speaks of a young sous chef working his

way up the line, filling a knife kit with the items that might one day define a career. A Depression-glass juicer inherited from a grandmother offers the thread of a tale about how one chef strives to bring grace and dignity to the workplace.

Throughout the book, the chefs describe a piece in their arsenal while also digging into their own histories. Cast iron skillets and wooden spoons, knives, graters, and stand mixers—these stories offer insight into life beyond the kitchen.

In this compilation, you'll find a collection of love letters. The stories will take you on journeys to the heart of the Midwest, out to a seafood market in

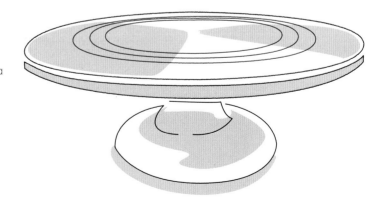

> *From biscuits to mussels to pig face thit kho, the dishes crisscross the American landscape and give a glimpse into the heart of each chef.*

Japan, to a stovetop in rural Vermont, to the Michelin-starred restaurants of New York and Paris, and, many times, to the famed Parisian kitchenware store, E.Dehillerin, where copper glimmers from every corner and just about every tool imaginable beckons from a box or a crate.

And while the tools themselves share special memories, what you'll also find is how often a chef will identify her or himself by the tools they use. Their descriptors define their implements, yes, but often capture the person using it, too. Sturdy. Efficient. Perfectly suited to its task. In many ways, the chefs are defining the traits they see—and feel pride for—within themselves.

Along with each story comes a recipe that speaks to a cooking style. Whether it's a dish passed down through family or a direct expression of what a chef prepares on his or her nightly menu, each exhibits a defining style of food. From biscuits to mussels to pig face thit kho, the dishes crisscross the American landscape and give a glimpse into the heart of each chef. My hope is that the stories and recipes you find here provide an insightful companion for anyone who enjoys being in the kitchen, surrounded by the tools that they love.

Erin Byers Murray

Erin Byers Murray received the 2015 M.F.K. Fisher Award for Excellence in Culinary Writing, awarded by Les Dames d'Escoffier, and is the author of *Shucked: Life on a New England Oyster Farm* and the James Beard nominated *The New England Kitchen.*

CONICAL STEAMER

Andrew Zimmern
Creator/Producer/Host of *Bizarre Foods with Andrew Zimmern*
Minneapolis, Minnesota

If you have yet to become a fan of sticky rice (*oryza sativa* for you Latin geeks), let me sing its praises. The short grain rice, also called glutinous rice, is actually gluten-free and grown mainly in southern and eastern Asia; it is a staple food in that part of the world. I love it served "boudin" style in fermented Thai, Khmer, or Viet sausages, and in Vietnamese desserts with pandan leaves or super-sweet grilled bananas. The Assamese use it in all their sweets. In Cambodia it's a standard breakfast item. The Burmese cook theirs in banana leaves with peas and have dozens of dishes centered around the stuff; it's even a big player during their New Year festival. The Chinese grind it and use it for wrappers and dumplings most famously eaten during the Dragon Boat Festival. The Filipinos cook it in coconut or banana leaves, topped with sweet or savory foods and call it *suman*. The Japanese use it for *mochi*.

Most importantly, it is the best, most amazing go-to starch for sopping up any Asian sauce or condiment. When the Italians invented Italian food and developed the notion of *scarpetta*—the last swab of the plate with your last nubbin of bread—what they really wished they had was sticky rice. I could

go on and on, but where everything stops stone cold is the presence of the stuff in American kitchens.

This grain is especially sticky when steamed because it's so low in amylose, which is what makes rice so starchy, and has a mother lode of amylopectin, which is what makes rice gluey, in a good way. It's a natural cultivar traceable to a single mutation that farmers jumped all over years ago. And yes, there is a super-sexy set of black, pink, and purple glutinous rices—if that's how you need to express yourself. You can roll this chewy, tensile grain into a ball with your hands to mop up all the leftover sauce on your plate. Skip utensils altogether and mold a morsel with your thumb into a spoon-sized vessel and use it to scoop up your food. Try soaking it in pure, sweetened coconut milk and topping

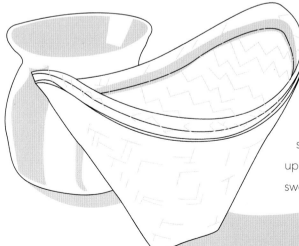

it with fresh mango slices for one of the world's best desserts. No matter how you use it, sticky rice adds a fun play-with-your-food element to dinner that both kids and adults can rally behind.

But there's a catch: If you want great sticky rice, it needs to soak and cook properly. The most important tool is the cooking vessel itself. Well, actually it's two pieces: a conical bamboo basket that fits snugly into an hourglass-shaped metal steaming pot, typically made of aluminum. If you use a conical basket like this, you'll have perfect rice every time. They are cheap, easy to find, and beautiful to look at. The baskets are woven and neatly pleated; they rinse clean without soap; and best of all, after a few uses they begin to take on the

> *If you use a conical basket like this, you'll have perfect rice every time. They are cheap, easy to find, and beautiful to look at.*

nutty, woodsy aroma of the rice, and the gentle scorch from the heat source you use. After I make the rice, I let it cool but always serve it warm or room temperature. I keep sticky rice in a small woven rice basket made of bamboo that I line with cheesecloth. It will sit for a day or two as we use up the whole batch, scooping and dipping, dunking and wondering why the Italians only use bread for their *scarpetta*.

STICKY RICE *with* PEANUT DIPPING SAUCE & BLACK BEAN DIPPING SAUCE

Courtesy of Andrew Zimmern • Serve 4 to 6

Sticky Rice

2 cups Thai sticky rice (glutinous rice)

Water

Peanut Sauce

½ cup dry-roasted peanuts (unsalted)

3 teaspoons peanut oil

6 cloves garlic, minced

⅓ cup ham or cooked bacon, very finely diced

⅓ cup toban Djan (fermented chile bean paste, try Lee Kum Kee brand)

½ cup tamarind puree

2-3 cups chicken stock

7 teaspoons sugar

1 or 2 Thai chiles, minced

Lime juice to taste

This often-overlooked starch—best cooked with a conical steamer—is to Asian sauces what biscuits are to a good sausage gravy. In this recipe it's served with two dishes of sauce—peanut and black bean—with sliced cucumbers on the side.

STICKY RICE

Place the rice in a large bowl and cover with water by 4 inches. Soak overnight.

Drain well and place the rice in a conical steaming basket (or in a damp muslin-lined sieve) set over a pot of boiling water. Cover the rice with a damp cloth. Do not let the bottom of the sieve touch the water.

Steam for 25 minutes. Let the rice rest for 10 minutes. Turn the rice out into a bowl and immediately cover with a warm, damp cloth.

PEANUT SAUCE

Using a mortar and pestle (or a food processor), crush the peanuts to a coarse powder; set aside.

Heat the oil in a large wok over high heat. Add the garlic and stir-fry until it begins to brown, about 15 seconds. Add bacon or ham, and cook for about 1 minute. Add the bean paste and tamarind puree, and stir to blend.

Add ½ cup of stock and most of the ground peanuts, reserving a few tablespoons for garnish. Stir in the sugar and

Black Bean Sauce

2 tablespoons peanut oil

3 whole dried red chiles

1 pound pork shoulder, finely diced

1¼ cups finely sliced leeks

1 cup minced scallions

1½ cups Chinese salted black beans (not the seasoned variety)

¾ cup hoisin

¾ cup oyster sauce

½ cup whole smashed and peeled garlic cloves

¾ cup soy sauce

1 cup dark brown sugar

½ cup golden syrup

3 cups hot water

3 cups chicken stock

Soy sauce to taste

Brown sugar to taste

To Serve

Sticky Rice

Peanut Sauce

Black Bean Sauce

2 cucumbers, sliced

minced chiles. Add more stock slowly until you have a thick but pourable (not watery) liquid. Simmer for 1 minute, then remove from heat. Season with lime juice to taste.

BLACK BEAN SAUCE

Place a large cast iron pot or heavy enameled casserole over high heat. Add the oil and swirl.

Add the chiles and swirl to brown on all sides. Do not burn or blacken. Add the pork and brown lightly. Add the leeks, scallions, and black beans. Cook for 1 to 2 minutes, then add all remaining ingredients.

Bring to a strong simmer, and stir for 3 to 5 minutes. Cover and reduce the heat to low; cook for 70 minutes, stirring occasionally. Take a peek. The sauce should be a rich consistency, and if need be, can be simmered more at this point. Adjust for salt (soy) or sweetness (sugar).

TO SERVE

Portion the sticky rice on plates or serve family style. Place the peanut sauce and black bean sauce in small serving dishes. Serve with the sliced cucumbers.

AN OLD
COLANDER

Jeremy Sewall

Chef / Owner of Lineage Restaurant; Chef / Partner
of Island Creek Oyster Bar and Row 34; Consulting
Chef of Eastern Standard Kitchen and Drinks

Boston, Massachusetts

For most of my childhood and into my twenties, I remember my grandmother using a colander with string handles while picking lettuces and vegetables in her gardens. She was from Maine and the wife of a lobsterman—a summer garden was an important part of living and, some years, surviving.

I can picture the colander in the yard just sitting there waiting to receive whatever was being picked— usually berries, green beans, or greens. It struck me as odd because the handles had long since broken off and she had used some string to fashion new ones. It served as a reminder that nothing was wasted. Broken handles were no reason to get rid of an otherwise useful colander.

It's been a long time since my grandparents have passed and the gardens were long ago planted over with grass. But recently, I somehow found myself the owner of this old colander. My wife asked for years if she could get rid of it—it stands out as a pale, old tool in a kitchen full of new stainless pans and gadgets. But I always said no because it was my grandmother's. Finally, about ten years ago, she stopped asking.

I don't have much of a garden, but we do grow lots of herbs and little tomatoes. I always

I always send my kids out with the old colander to pick basil for dinner or to collect the few ripe tomatoes that might be ready.

send my kids out with the old colander to pick basil for dinner or to collect the few ripe tomatoes that might be ready.

It is not the most useful tool in the kitchen, but what it does is remind me of some of the best values that anyone can have when they approach their food. Don't be wasteful. Things freshly picked are always better. Remember the effort your farmers put in to growing things for you and always be respectful of that. But mostly it reminds me of how my love for food started in a garden with an old colander.

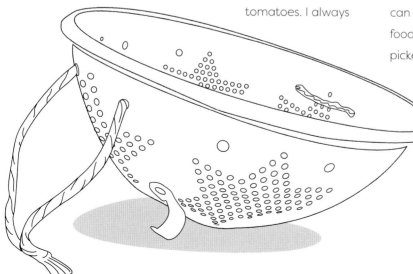

POLE BEAN & MEDLEY TOMATO SALAD

Courtesy of Jeremy Sewall • Serves 4

Vinaigrette

¼ cup champagne vinegar

1 small clove garlic

1 teaspoon fresh thyme leaves

2 teaspoons Dijon mustard

1 cup extra virgin olive oil

Salt and pepper to taste

Salad

2 cups pole beans (green and yellow), washed and cut in thirds on a bias

2 large shallots, peeled and roasted (see note)

¼ cup goats milk feta, crumbled

3 cups medley tomatoes, washed and cut in half or quarters

1 cup baby arugula

½ cup fresh basil leaves, as small as possible

Sea salt and freshly ground black pepper to taste

The key to this recipe is great tomatoes and beans right from the garden or a farmers' market. Be sure to use your colander to rinse everything off under cold water before you prep the ingredients.

VINAIGRETTE

Place the vinegar, garlic, thyme, and mustard in a blender and puree. Slowly add the olive oil to create an emulsion. Season with salt and pepper. Refrigerate until ready to use.

SALAD

Blanch the beans in boiling salted water and then place in ice water to stop the cooking. Once cold, drain and let dry. Remove the outer layer of skin from the roasted shallots and slice into thin rings. In a large mixing bowl, add half of the feta, along with the beans, tomatoes, shallots, arugula, and basil. Toss with just enough of the vinaigrette to lightly cover the vegetables. Carefully arrange on a platter. Drizzle a little more of the vinaigrette over the top and sprinkle with the rest of the feta; season with sea salt and pepper.

Note: To roast shallots, wrap whole, unpeeled shallots tightly in foil and roast at 400°F for about 15 minutes, or until shallots are soft. Let cool before unwrapping and peeling.

KNIFE BLOCK

Jonathan Benno
Executive Chef of Lincoln Ristorante
New York, New York

My father is retired now, but he was a carpenter. That's really where I got my work ethic, certainly, as well as my attention to detail. As a kid, it didn't matter if I was doing my homework or cleaning my room, my father would always say, "If you're going to do it, do it right." In his mind, there was no half-assed anything; you always did your best. I grew up watching him create things, build things. And still today, we'll go down to North Carolina to visit him and he's so meticulous, so precise, and so mindful about everything that he does. That's my dad, the carpenter.

When we were opening Per Se, my father wasn't involved in the construction of the restaurant, but I knew I wanted something that he built to be a part of the kitchen. At The French Laundry, Thomas Keller had all of these custom-sized boxes built for the very delicate pieces of china the restaurant used. To keep on with the tradition, we had my dad build some of those for Per Se. But I really wanted him to build something specifically for the kitchen, and somehow we arrived at the idea of a knife block. He built five, one for each of the opening sous chefs at Per Se.

The blocks are beautiful; they're made from oak and sit about four or five inches off a surface. They each have a dozen slots for knives

> *I really wanted my dad to build something specifically for the kitchen, and somehow we arrived at the idea of a knife block. He built five, one for each of the opening sous chefs at Per Se.*

and the whole piece is so balanced and perfectly aligned. There are no fixtures visible, so it's just very clean and functional—and completely one-of-a-kind. Of course, I've moved on from Per Se, and so have others. Those knife blocks are all over the country right now—one still lives at Per Se, and there's one at The French Laundry. I keep mine in my office at Lincoln. So every day, I'm reminded of my dad, as well as my time at Per Se.

CONIGLIO *in* "PORCHETTA"

Courtesy of Jonathan Benno • Serves 6 as an appetizer

Rabbit Mousse

7 teaspoons kosher salt

3 teaspoons pink curing salt

1 teaspoon sugar

5 cups rabbit meat

1 tablespoon potato starch

1 cup egg whites (from about 8 eggs)

2½ cups heavy cream

Special Equipment: Meat grinder

Rabbit Cylinders

2 whole rabbits, de-boned (butchers will debone upon request)

7 tablespoons Rabbit Mousse

1½ cups braised rabbit meat, cut in uniform dice

1 tablespoon black truffle, minced.

1 tablespoon Dijon mustard

2 tablespoons bacon fat

Barolo vinegar, to taste

Put your knife skills to the test and stun your tastebuds with this rabbit stuffed and rolled in the style of a porchetta.

RABBIT MOUSSE

Combine the kosher salt, pink curing salt, and sugar to create a "foie" cure. Reserve 1 tablespoon of cure; set aside remaining cure. Then fill a large bowl with ice and place a medium-sized bowl over it. Grind the rabbit meat through the small die of a meat grinder into the iced bowl. Place the ground meat in a food processor and add 1 tablespoon cure and potato starch.

Puree until the meat is a fine paste. Add the egg whites and puree until very smooth. Add the cream in a steady stream. Once the mixture is emulsified, transfer to a metal bowl. Cover with plastic wrap and refrigerate until ready to use.

RABBIT CYLINDERS

Finely score the rabbit meat with a sharp knife and lightly pound the inside of the belly flaps with a meat mallet. In a bowl, combine the mousse, braised meat, and black truffle. Spread half of the filling over the meat of one rabbit. Pull the flaps over to form a cylinder. Repeat the process with the second rabbit. Secure each rabbit with 3 pieces of butcher twine. Wrap in plastic to form a tight cylinder and tie the ends.

In a large, shallow pot, prepare a water bath to cover the rabbit cylinders by 1 to 2 inches. Heat the water to 160°F

(continued on next page)

CONIGLIO *in* "PORCHETTA" *(continued)*

Lentil Vinaigrette

1 cup green lentils

4 cups water

1 bouquet garni (2 sprigs parsley, 2 sprigs rosemary, and 1 bay leaf tied together with kitchen twine)

Salt and freshly ground pepper, to taste

1½ cups parsley, blanched and shocked

3 tablespoons roasted garlic, mashed

1½ cups baby spinach

2 tablespoons extra virgin olive oil, plus more to taste

2 tablespoons bacon fat

1 tablespoon Dijon mustard

Barolo vinegar (or red wine vinegar), to taste

To Serve

6 cups frisee

Borolo vinegar (or red wine vinegar), to taste

Extra virgin olive oil, to taste

Salt and freshly ground black pepper, to taste

6 whole eggs

Lentil Vinegarette

(test with a candy thermometer). Add the rabbit cylinders (still in plastic wrap) and poach, maintaining 160°F water temperature until the rabbit reaches 140°F. Shock the cylinders in an ice bath and refrigerate until ready to serve.

LENTIL VINAIGRETTE

In a large pot, combine the lentils with water and bouquet garni. Bring to a boil, then lower heat and simmer until tender. Remove the bouquet, drain, and season with salt and pepper. Reserve 6 tablespoons of lentils; put aside remaining lentils.

In a blender, combine blanched parsley, roasted garlic, baby spinach, and olive oil. Puree until smooth. Reserve 2 tablespoons of puree; put aside remaining puree. Combine the 6 tablespoons lentils with 2 tablespoons parsley puree, bacon fat, Dijon, Barolo vinegar, salt, pepper, and olive oil.

TO SERVE

Place the frisee in a large bowl and dress with Barolo vinegar, olive oil, salt, and pepper to taste. Set aside.

Heat a large sauté pan over medium-high heat and crack six eggs into the pan, cooking them sunny-side up.

To serve, slice the rabbit cylinders into 12 equal slices. Season each with olive oil, salt, and pepper. On each plate, spoon 1 tablespoon of Lentil Vinaigrette. Place 2 slices of rabbit porchetta on each plate. Place one fried egg on each plate offset from rabbit and lentils. Scatter frisee around each plate.

SWITCHBLADE
& POCKETKNIFE

Jonathon Sawyer

Chef / Owner of The Greenhouse Tavern, Trentina, Tavern Vinegar Company
Cleveland, Ohio

T he Kershaw assisted opening stainless steel switch blade is a tool that I use for just about anything and everything at the restaurants—sharpening pencils to write recipes and jot down menu ideas in my journal, tearing open boxes of sable fish or Saskatoon berries, segmenting lemons on the fly. Kershaw also makes Shun knives, so you know the blade is always at the ready, always sharp.

All of our corporate level team members carry one—in fact, we call the knife our "business card." Funny little story about that: As we were opening The Greenhouse Tavern, a ton of annoying solicitors would come by. The joke

> *From cutting open the papillote, to slicing a thin piece of lemon skin to burn and garnish the dish, it's a tool that I honestly couldn't get by without.*

fish. From cutting open the papillote, to slicing a thin piece of lemon skin to burn and garnish the dish, it's a tool that I honestly couldn't get by without. I also use it when making our wood-fired chop. For that, I cut a steel or marble slab just slightly larger than the protein being cooked, and sear the protein, as if on a plancha. The juices drip down creating both a beautiful smoke and this awesome wood-fired grill taste.

was that we would say, "Oh yeah, let me just go get you a business card" (aka, our knife!).

I use the blade when cooking a number of things, like our sustainable

SUSTAINABLE FISH *EN PAPIER*

Courtesy of Jonathon Sawyer • Serves 2

½ gallon water

2 tablespoons sea salt, plus more to taste

1 bottle (750 ml) Chablis or white burgundy

2 1½-pound lobsters

2 globe artichokes, peeled, turned, soaked, and purged

2 ounces fresh wild mushrooms (Hen of the Woods or other)

6 fingerling potatoes

Two 4-ounce fillets farm-raised Sturgeon (preferably sustainably harvested; skinless)

Parchment paper cut into two large pieces

1 tablespoon fresh lemon thyme leaves

4 tablespoons cultured butter

2 lemons, zested and sliced, preferably Meyer

Fleur de sel

This is a classic technique that is foolproof for fish cookery at home. This dish was also a huge hit on the opening menu at The Greenhouse Tavern. All the steps up to the assembly stage can be done a day or two in advance. Feel free to improvise on the ingredients.

In a large pot over medium heat, combine the water, 2 tablespoons sea salt, and ¾ of the bottle of Chablis. Bring to a low simmer, then add the whole lobsters and simmer until cooked, about 7 minutes. Remove lobsters from the pot and refrigerate. Once the lobster is cool, remove the meat from the shell and slice into 1-inch pieces.

Note: Artichokes are fickle and can be tricky unless treated properly. Start with enough water to cover the artichokes and add 2 tablespoons of salt and 2 tablespoons of vinegar. Let soak for about 20 to 30 minutes and rinse under hot water for a few minutes before cooking.

In the same pot over medium heat, poach the artichokes until cooked through, about 22 minutes. Remove artichokes from the pot and refrigerate. Once cool, slice into 1-inch thick pieces.

In the same pot over medium heat, poach the wild mushrooms until cooked through, about 12 minutes. Remove from the pot and refrigerate. Once cool, slice into 1-inch thick pieces.

(continued on next page)

SUSTAINABLE FISH *EN PAPIER* (continued)

In the same pot over medium heat, poach the new potatoes until cooked through, about 17 minutes. Remove from the pot and refrigerate. Once cool, slice into 1-inch thick pieces. Reserve the poaching liquid and let cool.

ASSEMBLY

Heat the oven to 350°F.

Season all of the ingredients, including the sturgeon fillets, with a drizzle of extra virgin olive oil and sea salt. On each piece of parchment paper, place a couple of slices of potato, some wild mushrooms, slices of artichokes, a few pieces of lobster, one fillet of fish, 2 slices of Meyer lemon, a sprinkle of lemon thyme, and a pat of butter. Fold the sides of the parchment paper up to create a shallow vessel. Add 2 ounces of the cooled poaching liquid to each package. Continue folding the edges of the parchment square over themselves to seal the package.

Place the packages on a baking sheet and bake until the fish is just cooked through, about 10 to 15 minutes. The broth will be bubbling at this point. Let the packages rest for a few minutes before opening.

Once opened, drizzle with extra virgin olive oil, Meyer lemon zest, and fleur de sel.

COPPER-BOTTOM
REVERE WARE POTS

Sarah Schafer
Executive Chef of Irving Street Kitchen
Portland, Oregon

M y great grandfather and great grandmother lived in Buffalo, New York. He was a butcher and she was an amazing cook—she's actually the reason why I cook. Years after my great grandmother passed away, we went to visit my Grandmother Ernst, who told me that there was a box in the garage for me. Apparently, my great grandmother had been very specific about who got what. Inside the box were all of her Revere Ware pots and pans. They're made of steel but the bottoms are pure copper—nowadays everything has a layer of steel and then a layer of copper in the middle. But with these, you have to be a seasoned cook in order to know how to control the heat. She took pristine care of them, washing them by hand every night and making sure the copper was properly polished.

Photograph courtesy of Sarah Schafer

I remember her cooking with those pots and being in her kitchen. She used to make a chicken soup that was such a nourishing broth that you could feel every bone in your body getting better as you ate it. She was also the kind of woman who knew how to hang wallpaper or reupholster a chair. She could do just about anything . . . and then she would drink a beer afterwards. Just a really cool woman and way before her time. When I was really young, I used to tell her that I wished that we were the same age so that we could do everything together.

> *My great grandmother took pristine care of them, washing them by hand every night and making sure the copper was properly polished.*

Every once in a while I try to make her soup—but I can't for the life of me make it like she does. There's always something that's missing. Sometimes I wonder if it's because of who is cooking it. I know her recipe and what she used put into it, but I feel like there's something she didn't write down. Like there's something that isn't quite true to the marrow of what she did.

Sometimes, when you're surrounded by food and cooking constantly, you can lose interest in cooking at home. But when I cook with my great grandmother's pots, it reminds me of why I love cooking.

GREAT GRANDMA'S CHICKEN SOUP

Courtesy of Sarah Schafer • Serves 4 to 6

1 whole chicken, deboned; meat and carcass reserved

1-2 pounds raw beef bones

1 pound chicken necks and gizzards

2 tablespoons salt, plus more to taste

¼ cup apple cider vinegar

4 large carrots, roughly chopped

4 large celery stalks, roughly chopped

4 large leeks, roughly chopped

4 large onions, roughly chopped

Several sprigs of thyme, tied together with butcher's twine

If you can rely on only one cooking credo, it's that the best chicken soup is passed down from the hand of a grandmother. Filling a large pot with raw beef bones puts a unique spin on this otherwise classic recipe.

Cut the reserved chicken meat into 1-inch cubes and refrigerate. Chop up the chicken carcass and place in a large soup kettle. Add the beef bones, necks, and gizzards. Cover with water by 2 inches. Add the salt and vinegar. Bring to a simmer and let bubble for 10 to 15 minutes, skimming off surface scum that forms on top.

Add half of each of the vegetables, plus the herb bouquet to the broth. Return to a simmer and cook for 3 to 4 hours; be careful not to bring to a full boil. Continue to skim, skim, and skim until the broth is rich and clear. Add water as needed to keep the bones covered.

Once the broth is flavorful to taste, strain and reserve the liquid. In a large saucepan, add the diced chicken and remaining vegetables. Pour the strained broth over the meat and vegetables and bring to a simmer. Let simmer until the chicken is cooked through. Season with salt to taste, and serve.

BAKER'S SPATULA

Kyle Mendenhall
Executive Chef of The Kitchen Restaurants
Boulder, Colorado

I found this particular spatula about five years ago at a swap meet in a very small town in Wisconsin called Viroqua—my wife's family has a dairy farm there that's been in the family for over 100 years. We go there just about every year and every time we go, I make sure to check out the swap meet—at least that's what I call it. It's set in this giant hall and folks come to sell their things and everyone has their own little cubby. There's always so much weird, random stuff but there are also old kitchen tools everywhere. I found this baker's spatula there and realized that it has to be at least a hundred years old—it was made by a company called Nichols Bros., which was out of Greenfield, Massachusetts, but the company shut down in the 1920s.

Photograph courtesy of Sarah Schafer

It's not quite an offset spatula—this one is actually straight and flat and two inches from the end, I gave it just a little bend, which helps when I use it to get into things. Plus, it's thinner than most spatulas, which makes it more flexible. It's the one thing that I always make sure I have in my knife bag. I travel a lot and try to travel pretty light so I bring one important knife, a couple of my favorite spoons, and this spatula.

As a chef, I don't work the line as much as I used to—I'm more toward the guidance counselor end of things these days—but I find that there are these moments of Zen when I'm setting up my station or getting my *mise en place* ready. I always want to be as tidy, small, and efficient as possible. I don't want to have ten tools on my station. This spatula, it's not too big or wide but it works for *everything*, from turning a hamburger to doing something more delicate like cooking fish. You never want to

> *I found this baker's spatula and realized that it has to be at least a hundred years old—it was made by a company called Nichols Bros., which was out of Greenfield, Massachusetts, but the company shut down in the 1920s.*

touch fish with a pair of tongs so you need something that has a little bit more finesse—this is actually the perfect size for cooking scallops. But really, I like having it around because it's so versatile that it allows me the ability to work simply.

DIVER SCALLOPS *with* LARDED LENTILS

Courtesy of Kyle Mendenhall • Serves 4

1 cup Le Puy green lentils

1 bay leaf

Kosher salt

1 teaspoon olive oil

4 ounces lardo, diced small (look for La Quercia brand, or substitute fat back)

2 carrots, diced small

1 leek, diced small

1 small celery root, diced small

1 tablespoon minced garlic

1 tablespoon sherry vinegar

16 diver sea scallops (preferably from Maine)

1 tablespoon canola oil

2 tablespoons butter, divided

1 cup chopped radicchio

Fresh diver scallops are handpicked and worth the extra cost. They also present an unexpected use for your baker's spatula.

Rinse the lentils by swirling in cold water and draining. In a large pot, cover the lentils with water and add the bay leaf. Bring to a boil, skimming off foam that rises to the surface, then turn the heat to low and cover. Cook for 15 minutes; check for doneness. Lentils should not be fully cooked but slightly al dente. Season with the salt, drain, and set aside.

In a large sauté pan, heat the olive oil and add the lardo, sautéing over low heat until the lardo fat is rendered. Add the vegetables and garlic and season with salt. Cook for 4 to 5 minutes; the vegetables should remain al dente. Add the sherry vinegar, then immediately remove from the heat. In a large bowl, combine the lentils with the vegetables; set aside.

Pat the scallops with a towel until very dry. Season with a good pinch of salt on both sides. Add the canola oil to a large sauté pan over high heat. Once the pan is very hot, place the scallops gently in the pan. Cook until the scallops are well browned and caramelized on one side. Add a tablespoon of butter and, using a baker's spatula, turn the scallops. Remove from heat and baste the scallops with the butter in the pan.

Place the lentil mixture and a little water in a saucepan and re-warm over low heat. Add 1 tablespoon of butter and the chopped radicchio; stir to combine. Adjust seasoning to taste. Top the lentils with the scallops, served caramelized side up.

CHASSEUR
SAUTÉ PAN

Robert Wiedmaier
Chef/Owner of Marcel's
Washington D.C.

T he key essential piece of cookware that I need in all of my kitchens is the Chasseur. Chasseur is a French brand of enameled cast iron cookware and trivets that was established almost a century ago in France. The term is French for "hunter" but is also a designation given to certain regiments of French and Belgian light infantry.

All of my establishments reflect my European heritage, in particular my link to Belgium. I was born in Germany to a Belgian father and Californian mother who was a great cook—she could make anything from anything.

At our house growing up, we didn't have this particular brand, but a more rustic version that got beaten up quite a lot because it was one of the main cooking pieces in our household—we used it for almost everything. I can remember walking home from school, and just barely reaching the door before smelling the mussels as they got their dose of cream, wine, and herbs—the aroma was so strong. It meant it was a special occasion, as we did not have mussels that often. It was a delicacy for us. My father was in the military, so mussels were not something that we could purchase on a tight budget. But we didn't need to add much to make them special—we made them in the traditional manner. Just having them was good enough for me and my family.

> *I can remember walking home from school, and just barely reaching the door before smelling the mussels as they got their dose of cream, wine, and herbs.*

At the restaurant, we not only cook with a Chasseur, but we serve our mussels in its colorful enamel at the table. It steams the mussels perfectly and the cast iron retains the heat to maintain the constant warm temperature if lingering over a meal with family and friends. Mussels are a dish I serve at my restaurants in many styles and seasonings to be readily available at all times. No one should *not* have mussels, especially for the sauce alone after the juices of the ocean ooze into the seasonings. I say, pass the bread!

BLUE BAY MUSSELS PROVENÇAL

Courtesy of Robert Wiedmaier • Serves 2 to 4

1 tablespoon unsalted butter

1 tablespoon minced garlic

1 tablespoon minced shallot

1 pound Blue Bay mussels, cleaned and debearded, in the shell

1 cup dry vermouth

1 cup heavy cream

1 tablespoon fresh flat-leaf parsley, chopped

Crusty bread

When you start with fresh, live mussels, much of the cook's job is to simply stay out of their way. Here they are sauteéd in vermouth, heavy cream, and fresh herbs, a decadent sauce that begs to be soaked up with thick, crusty bread.

Place a Chasseur sauté pan or other heavy pan over medium heat and add the butter. Sweat the garlic and shallot until translucent, about 45 to 60 seconds. Add the mussels and vermouth, and cover the pot. When the mussels are almost open (about 90 seconds to 2 minutes), add the heavy cream and cover the pot. Once all of the mussels are open (about 2 more minutes), sprinkle parsley over top and serve with crusty bread. Discard any mussels that don't open.

Cooked mussels can be eaten directly from the pot or pan or transferred to a wide-rimmed soup bowl. Keep covered until just prior to eating as they cool quickly.

CAST IRON PAN & SILVER SPOON

Rob Newton
Chef/Owner of Wilma Jean and Nightingale 9
Brooklyn, New York

For me, it comes down to the essentials: a cast iron pan and a silver spoon. The first is my Grandma's cast iron pan that I was given about ten years ago. My grandma, who grew up in the Ozarks of Arkansas, had this cast iron pan for most of her adult life, and it was extremely well cared for. For more than fifty years, the pan frequently saw pork chops, potatoes, and poke salad, depending on the time of the year. The one item that was most often in the pan was her cornbread, and that is what has given this pan such a beautiful finish. Bacon fat can have that effect. I continue this tradition today and care for it properly after every use. This vintage cast iron pan and its nonstick finish, accomplished after many decades of use, is truly a family heirloom and probably my most treasured piece of kitchen equipment.

Another item that most chefs find indispensible are favorite spoons that we tend to carry around with us. The most common is probably the "Kunz" spoon, named for the uber talented chef Gray Kunz. These spoons can be found in most kitchens. Tweezers are quite common in kitchens these days as well, but it is hard to actually taste food with them, therefore, I prefer spoons for tasting and plating. This silver spoon came into my life about

The one item that was most often in the pan was my Grandma's cornbread, and that is what has given this pan such a beautiful finish. Bacon fat can have that effect.

20 years ago from a restaurant that has since closed and I keep it as a reminder of a time when I didn't have a clue about real cooking but kept my head down and continued to learn. So far, so good.

MY DAD'S FRIED CORN

Courtesy of Rob Newton • Serves 4 to 6

6 ears sweet corn (or 1 to 1½ ears of fresh corn per person)

4 tablespoons bacon fat

Salt to taste

10-12 cranks on a peppermill of black pepper

¼ cup chicken stock or water

3 sprigs fresh thyme, leaves picked from stems

"This dish always needs a little explanation because it's not deep fried, as we know it in modern terms," Newton says. *"My family calls this fried corn because it is cooked in a little grease (aka: bacon fat) in a hot skillet and 'fried' in the pan."*

Peel away the outer layers and silk of the corn. Hold a clean ear of corn upright in a bowl and carefully slice the kernels into the bowl. Be careful not to cut too deeply into the cob, as this will scrape off the corn milk (see below).

Once all of the kernels are removed, turn the knife to use the dull edge and scrape the corncob from top to bottom, releasing the corn milk from the cob into the same bowl. Repeat with remaining corn. Combine the kernels and milk; discard the cobs.

Heat your best cast iron skillet over high heat and add the bacon fat. Once the fat is shimmering and just beginning to smoke, add the corn and stir once or twice. Keep the flame high and spread the corn evenly in the pan. (Be careful: kernels may pop.) Season with salt and pepper and cook 1 minute longer before stirring again. Reduce the heat slightly and stir one more time; corn should start to brown on the bottom. Add the stock and stir, removing any brown bits; cook for 1 to 2 more minutes. Remove from the heat and transfer to a serving dish. Sprinkle thyme leaves over top and serve.

BISCUIT CUTTER

Tandy Wilson
Executive Chef and Owner of City House
Nashville, Tennessee

I got this biscuit cutter from my mom, who got it from Nana Crick—her name was Christine but we called her Nana Crick. It maybe started as a can of sweet potatoes or milk—it could have been anything. But it was just the right size and it was a smooth metal can that she poked a hole in the top of.

I've always had this desire to feed people—I just want to put big plates of food in front of people all the time, and I'm pretty sure this gene came from her. And Nana Crick made good biscuits—she made them the way I like them, which is on the thinner side, where it's more about the top and bottom crust. I'm pretty sure the term "big fluffy biscuit" was a marketing term someone came up with in the '80s or '90s because

Photograph by Andrea Behrends

that's not really Southern food to me—it's not home cooking. Those big fluffy ones are more of a restaurant thing.

The biscuits I remember eating at home were thinner. And for a long time, anytime I hired anyone new, I would have to show them how to make biscuits because no matter how Southern they thought they were, I just didn't agree with most people's theories on how their biscuits should be made. But when I tasted our pastry chef Rebekah Turshen's biscuits, it was the first time I'd ever encountered one that was better than mine.

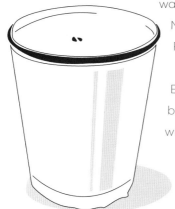

Now, I only ever use Rebekah's recipe.

Every Christmas Eve, we do a whole baked country ham, which my great aunt,

> *It maybe started as a can of sweet potatoes or milk—it could have been anything. But it was just the right size and it was a smooth metal can that she poked a hole in the top of.*

who came from the same side of family as Nana Crick, would do every year, too. We'd fry the center slices and that was our Christmas Eve tradition. I do mine with a three-day soak and bake it overnight and just put it on the table with a sorghum glaze on the back. Everybody has to drink a few extra glasses of water before bed but they all love it. And I always serve it with Rebekah's biscuits.

REBEKAH'S BUTTERMILK BISCUITS

Courtesy of Rebekah Turshen • Makes about 24 biscuits

8 ounces unsalted butter, chilled

600 grams (just shy of 5 cups) unbleached all-purpose flour

2 tablespoons baking powder

½ teaspoon baking soda

1 tablespoon large flat-grained kosher salt

2 cups whole-fat buttermilk

Those rise-to-the-sky restaurant biscuits aren't the norm in many Southern homes. These thinner biscuits, cut with an old repurposed metal can, are the perfect size for letting good country ham or fresh preserves shine.

Heat the oven to 450°F for a conventional oven or 425°F for a convection oven.

Cut the cold butter into pat-sized pieces. Cover and refrigerate again until firm. In a large bowl, combine the flour, baking powder, baking soda, and salt and mix with fingertips to eliminate any stray lumps of flour. Dump in the butter and toss with flour. With floured fingers, smash the butter pats into flat pieces. Once all of the butter is flattened, go through with fingertips again to break butter bits down to a half inch or so.

Fold in the buttermilk with a rubber spatula until the dough just begins to come together.

Dump the mixture out onto a floured board. Fold dough onto itself six or seven times. Roll out dough to ⅓- or ½-inch thickness. Using a 2½-inch biscuit cutter, punch out biscuits and bake 12 to 15 minutes until the tops are nicely toasted.

COPPER
JAM POT

Nicole Krasinski

**Pastry Chef / Proprietor of State
Bird Provisions and The Progress**
San Francisco, California

I had been a pastry chef for about seven years
before I'd even heard of copper jam pots. Maybe I'd
seen them mentioned in a recipe, but I didn't really
understand the necessity. And then a few years ago,
my friend Michelle Polzine, who runs the 20th Century
Café here in San Francisco, had one and we were
making jam at her house together and I saw what
a big difference it made in the final product. It gave
larger meaning to the task of making jam—something
about it just felt right, like when you have the right
tool for such a specialized task.

So I fell in love with the copper jam pot and even
though they're extremely expensive, that year, for my
37th birthday, Michelle found an antique one for me

and gave it to me as a gift. I think it came from France—it doesn't have any brand on it, or any indication of where it's from—but it was clearly very well taken care of by the previous owners. And it's the perfect size for a small batch of jam. The next year, I ended up buying my assistant one—it really is a great and thoughtful gift for anyone in the food world—and then I bought another one for myself.

The pots take on a really nice patina. They're short and wide and the sides go at an angle, meaning there's more surface area for the jam. If you run a spatula on, say, the bottom of a regular steel pot, you can feel a little bit of abrasion. If you run a spatula along the bottom of these pots, they're completely smooth, so when you're cooking jam you can feel when it's starting to stick, which is an indication that

> *The pots take on a really nice patina. They're short and wide and the sides go at an angle, meaning there's more surface area for the jam.*

it's almost done. Plus, there's no carryover cooking like in a steel pot so you really have a lot of control. I think that it produces more shininess in the final product and an overall retention of a bright fruit flavor. The end result is far superior.

Now we have three pots between us so we can produce a lot of jam, which we do in order to have plenty in the winter when there's no fresh fruit around. And, what's fun is that another chef friend of mine makes apricot jam at her house every year, so as soon as it's apricot season, she calls me and says, "Ok, I need the pot!" It's becoming a community tool, which is really very cool.

STRAWBERRY PLUM JAM

Courtesy of Nicole Krasinski · Fills 6 to 8 ½-pint jars

5½ cups granulated sugar

3 pints strawberries, washed
and hulled

3 pounds Santa Rosa plums, washed,
pitted, and cut into ¼-inch pieces

The perfect jam pot deserves the perfect jam. The combination of strawberry and plums lends this recipe just enough tartness to showcase the fruit flavor out front.

Combine the sugar and fruit in a bowl. Stir to completely coat the fruit in sugar, and let macerate at room temperature for at least 1½ hours, or up to 4 hours.

Pour the fruit into a copper pot and place over medium heat. As the fruit begins to cook, skim off any foam that forms on the surface. Turn the heat down to medium low and cook until thickened, stirring often with a spatula until it reaches 220°F on a candy thermometer. Pour the jam into a bowl to cool. Once it reaches room temperature, pour into jars and refrigerate for up to two weeks.

BONING KNIFE

Chris Shepherd
Owner / Executive Chef of Underbelly
Houston, Texas

In everyday life in the kitchen, there are many tools that you use to make the day a successful one. The one tool that makes my world go 'round is an easy one: my boning knife. It is the starting point of most things that happen daily.

I run a restaurant that is based on whole animal cooking. Every week we receive one 1,000-pound steer, three 250-pound pigs, one 200-pound goat, 700 pounds of whole fish, and an array of poultry. Everything must pass by the knife. It is the most worked tool there is, and it's priceless to me.

We butcher using an Austrian seam method where you cut around muscle when breaking down animals, not the traditional method of cutting through muscle.

This leaves us whole muscle to be able to further utilize the entire animal. It gives us the advantage of different cuts. Our philosophy is to respect the animal for giving us its life so that we can enjoy ours.

The boning knife must become one with your hand. It is a tool that has to be used properly, and it must also be respected. I, for one, know this well. Accidents do happen. I went through a feather bone on a pig once, and the knife went into my wrist. One precise cut, right through my artery.

I have a great respect for the art of butchering and the one major tool that is associated with it. Not all knives are

> *I have a great respect for the art of butchering and the one major tool that is associated with it. Not all knives are created equal.*

created equal, and choosing what works for you is important. The shape of the blade, length, thickness, flexibility. The handle must fit right. It's an extension of your body. I have used many different ones over my career, but I have found my style: medium length, slight upward curvature, firm flexibility, black plastic ergonomic handle. This is my choice, the one thing that I see on a daily basis.

I have become one with it.

PIG FACE THIT KHO

Courtesy of Chris Shepherd • Serves 4

2 tablespoons unsalted butter

2 yellow onions, thinly sliced

1 jalapeño, stemmed and sliced
    into rounds

4 whole star anise

2 cinnamon sticks

½ cup brown sugar

¼ cup fish sauce

3 cups pork stock, preferably
    homemade

4 medium carrots, cut into
    1-inch pieces

1-inch cubes of sous vide pig
    face (recipe follows)

Salt, to taste

Freshly ground black pepper to taste

1 baguette, sliced

Sous Vide Pig Face
Makes 1 whole pig face

1 pig head

Water

Salt

Sugar

Ice Bath

Specialty Equipment:
Immersion circulator

Hone your skills with a boning knife as you prep the meat for this savory Vietnamese stew.

Heat the butter in a large Dutch oven over medium-high heat. Add the onions and cook until soft, about 8 minutes. Stir periodically throughout the process, Add the jalapeño, star anise, and cinnamon and cook until fragrant, about 2 minutes. Add the brown sugar and cook until dissolved, about 2 minutes. Add the fish sauce and cook, scraping the bottom of the pan, about 1 minute. Pour in the stock and bring to a boil. Reduce the heat to medium-low and simmer, covered, about 20 minutes. Add the carrots and the cubes of meat (see below). Simmer uncovered for 15 minutes. Divide the stew among 4 bowls and serve with the sliced baguette.

SOUS VIDE PIG FACE

Clean the head thoroughly. Starting from under the mouth, make an incision and peel the flesh from the bone, working your way around the entire head. Once the flesh is removed, combine water, salt, and sugar and brine the face in it for 24 hours. Remove the face and pat dry. Roll up the head and place in a sous vide bag. Place the bag in an immersion circulator at 60°C. Leave in water bath for 48 hours. After 48 hours, place meat in an ice bath to chill. Heat the oven to 500°F. Cut chilled meat into 1-inch cubes. Place on a wire rack set in a rimmed baking sheet and cook 15 minutes, until crispy.

ANTIQUE CLEAVER

Steven Satterfield
Chef of Miller Union
Atlanta, Georgia

I inherited this antique cleaver about six or seven years ago—it's actually made by Wüsthof but it has some Japanese writing on it. I've never been able to trace the origins of it but it appears to be from the '50s or '60s and probably a collaboration of some sort for Wüsthof. It belonged to my partner's grandmother and when we were moving her to Atlanta from Augusta, Georgia, where she lived, his family found it and gave it to me. I'm not sure where she got a hold of it, but clearly it was well taken care of. I had it resharpened and contoured so it's got a little bit of a curve to the blade, almost like a mezzaluna.

There's something about the design of the handle and the brass that makes it feel like it's from a

Photograph by Heidi Geldhauser

different era—even the lettering used to spell "Wüsthof" is different, more block-like. There's some routing in the wood handle that gives it a distinctive look and the stainless steel blade is still fairly shiny, but there are a few scratches so you can see where it's been used a lot.

I use it quite a bit—we use different knives for specific functions but this one is great for vegetable prep, especially if you're cutting something heavy like fall squash or pumpkin. The knife itself is heavy—it can be interchangeable with a chef's knife—but because it's a cleaver it doesn't turn corners well. The blade is about 2½ inches wide, so it's not the knife I would use to supreme an orange—but it's fantastic for straight cuts and especially herbs.

> *There's something about the design of the handle and the brass that makes it feel like it's from a different era—even the lettering used to spell "Wüsthof" is different, more block-like.*

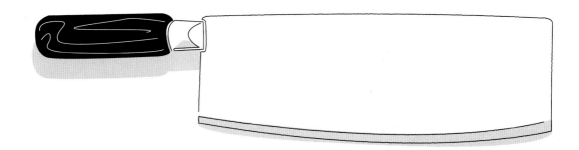

ROASTED BUTTERNUT SQUASH & APPLES

Courtesy of Steven Satterfield • Serves 4 to 6

1 large butternut squash (or 2 small)

1 red onion, cut into ½-inch dice

½ teaspoon each roughly chopped
fresh thyme, sage, and
rosemary leaves

2 tablespoons extra virgin olive oil

Kosher salt and freshly ground
black pepper

2 large or 3 small apples

2 tablespoons unsalted butter, melted

That heavy cleaver you seldom use is unexpectedly suited to cutting dense vegetables like apples and butternut squash. The two vegetables combine here for a hearty dish rich with the taste of fresh herbs.

Position two racks in the oven, one-third above the bottom and one-third below the top. Heat the oven to 375°F.

With a Y-shape peeler, remove the outer skin of the squash. With a long knife, slice off about ½ inch of the stem end and the base end. Place the squash base-side down on a cutting board, so that it stands up on its own. Carefully insert the blade of the knife across the diameter of the squash and slowly rock the knife until it is fully inserted. With both hands, carefully push down through the squash until your blade reaches the cutting board and the squash is bisected. Remove the seeds and discard or save for another use.

With each half-squash cut side down, separate the wider, hollow base from the solid upper section. Cut the hollow pieces lengthwise radially into long, 1-inch-wide strips. Trim each strip into 1-inch cubes. Cut the solid upper pieces into 1-inch cubes also. Place all of the cubed squash in a large mixing bowl. Add the onion, thyme, sage, rosemary, and olive oil. Season liberally with salt and a few turns of the pepper mill. Toss well to combine and transfer to a parchment-lined baking sheet. Roast until the squash is tender, 20 to 25 minutes.

(continued on next page)

ROASTED BUTTERNUT SQUASH & APPLES *(continued)*

While the squash is roasting, peel the apples. Slice the apples vertically into 4 equal quarters. Place each quarter cut side down, with the seeds facing your knife. With the blade at a 45-degree angle, slice away the core and the seeds from each quarter. Slice each quarter into three pieces lengthwise, then cut the pieces in half crosswise. Transfer the apples to a bowl, toss with melted butter, and season lightly with salt. Turn the apples out onto a parchment-lined baking sheet, and roast until the apples are tender, 10 to 15 minutes. When both the squash mixture and the apples have finished roasting, combine and taste for seasoning before serving.

METAL SKEWER

Stuart Brioza

Chef and Proprietor of State Bird Provisions and The Progress
San Francisco, California

I first started using a metal skewer when I was staging at the restaurant Michel Rostang in Paris. All of the cooks would temp their meats by using a skewer—they would stick the skewer through the roast, whether it was lamb or something larger, and then hold the skewer to the top of their bottom lip, rubbing it from side to side. They'd know the doneness of the meat by how warm the center of the skewer was. They didn't have to remember specific temperatures, it was all by feel. The first time I saw it I thought it was just awesome.

Later, I was over at E.Dehillerin, the mind-bendingly awesome cookware store in Paris, and saw the same types of skewers—I bought the whole box and started practicing. Once I nailed it and understood what to feel for, it really changed the game for me. I've been using metal skewers to temp meats ever since.

The ones I bought (I still have two from the original box) are about 10 inches long and 2 millimeters in diameter. A lot of cooks will use cake testers, but I find the gauge on the skewers to be a little better for holding the temperature. And it works with just about any big roast, like pork loin or a rack of lamb. It's also great for all sizes of poultry and even artichokes—I'll poke an artichoke while it's cooking to see how easily the skewer slides in and out.

Not to mention, it's really impressive when you show people how it works.

> *A lot of cooks will use cake testers, but I find the gauge on the skewers to be a little better for holding the temperature. And it works with just about any big roast, like pork loin or a rack of lamb.*

I teach all my cooks to temp meat this way, so my whole kitchen uses them now (often with a cork stuck in one end). When I'm teaching a cooking class, the big joke is that you'll know that your host has overcooked the meat if they come to the table with a blister on their lip.

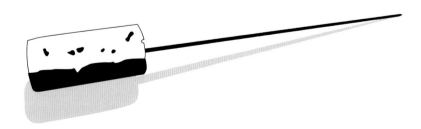

GRILLED BEEF *with* CHILE VINAIGRETTE *&* GARLIC CHIPS

Courtesy of Stuart Brioza • Serves 2

Chile Vinaigrette

⅓ cup fresh red chile juice
(preferably from Fresno chiles)

2 tablespoons fresh lime juice

2 teaspoons salt

⅓ cup grapeseed oil

Garlic Chips

10 cloves garlic, thinly sliced
on a mandoline

2 cups whole milk

Rice bran oil, for frying

A thick cut of strip loin allows you to get a thick sear on the outside, but when you cut into the steak you're looking for whatever level of doneness you prefer. With a little practice, you can learn to test doneness using metal skewers. Once done, delicately fried garlic chips and a spicy vinaigrette finish it off.

CHILE VINAIGRETTE

In a small mixing bowl, whisk all of the ingredients together. Reserve until ready to use.

GARLIC CHIPS

In a large pot, combine the garlic and whole milk. Bring the mixture to a simmer over low heat, stirring occasionally. Once it reaches a simmer, strain the mixture through a fine mesh sieve and rinse garlic with cold water until it runs clear. Transfer the garlic onto a paper towel-lined baking sheet to dry.

Pour enough oil into a medium pot to reach a depth of 2 inches. Set the pot over medium-high heat and bring the oil to 275°F. (Use a deep fry thermometer to gauge the temperature of the oil.) Add the garlic slices in batches so that they do not overcrowd the pot. Fry, turning the garlic over occasionally and adjusting the heat to maintain the oil's temperature, until the garlic slices are light golden brown and crispy. Transfer the pieces to a paper-towel-lined baking sheet. Reserve the chips until ready to use.

Grilled Beef

12 ounces beef strip loin (2 inches thick)

Kosher salt to taste

Vegetable oil

¼ cup scallions sliced on the bias

GRILLED BEEF

Prepare a grill or grill pan over high heat. Using paper towels, pat the strip loin dry and generously season all over with salt. Rub a touch of oil on the grill grate or pan. Grill the strip loin and cook to medium rare by testing the steak with a metal skewer. (Insert the skewer at an angle at the thickest part of the steak. Pull it out and rub it across the bottom of your lip. For the perfect medium rare, it should feel hot, then warm, and then hot again going from one end of the skewer to the other.)

Transfer the steak to a cutting board to rest for 10 minutes. Slice the steak against the grain into ½-inch thick slices.

In a serving dish, place the steak slices on the bottom and drizzle the chile vinaigrette over top. Garnish with garlic chips and scallions. Serve hot.

MEME'S
CAST IRON SKILLET

Virginia Willis
Southern Chef and Cookbook Author
Atlanta, Georgia

My maternal grandmother, whom I called Meme, was a great cook. She was famous for her buttery pound cake, yeast rolls, and her homemade jams and jellies. She was also famous for her fried chicken and buttermilk cornbread, both made in her ancient cast iron skillet. I am now the proud owner of that skillet and calculate that it may be nearly 100 years old. To say it's well seasoned is an understatement. It's black and shiny like satin and water beads on it when I wash it, the result of absorbing so much oil through the decades. I know it sounds cliché, but it's true: this cast iron skillet is hands-down my absolute most precious possession.

When I returned to the South from living in New York, it sat wrapped in a towel on the front seat of the car.

No one dared touch it. No one dared suggest it be relegated to the cardboard box for the movers. This simple kitchen tool is dearer to me than any other cooking equipment; indeed, it's dearer to me than any other thing I own. Clothes can be replaced, jewelry can be purchased, art can be painted. But nothing can come close to the link I feel to my grandmother when I hold this skillet.

While it rarely fries chicken on Sundays like it once did, I do use it daily. (Don't think I don't see the irony of cooking my own version of lightened up Southern food in a skillet that's likely fried an entire chicken house of

> *I carefully wash it in warm soapy water and dry it, and then I return it to the oven for keeping. This procedure is as much kitchen housekeeping as sacred ritual.*

hens.) I carefully wash it in warm soapy water and dry it, and then I return it to the oven for keeping. This procedure is as much kitchen housekeeping as sacred ritual. Not only is it my go-to pan, it's my kitchen totem. I feel connected to my food, my culture, my family, and my place when I hold the gently worn handle in my hand.

VEGETABLE CORN BREAD

Courtesy of Virginia Willis • Serves 8 to 10

2 tablespoons canola oil

2 cups yellow whole-grain cornmeal

1 teaspoon fine sea salt

1 teaspoon baking soda

6 fresh okra pods, stem ends trimmed, very thinly sliced (about 1 cup)

1 red onion, chopped

Cut and scraped kernels from 2 ears of fresh corn, cut from the cob (about 1 cup)

1 banana pepper, thinly sliced into rings

1 jalapeño chile, thinly sliced into rings

1 small red chile, such as bird's eye or Thai, thinly sliced into rings

½ poblano chile, cored, seeded, and chopped

2 cups low-fat buttermilk

1 large egg, lightly beaten

"The suggested vegetables here are just that," says Willis. *"Mix it up depending on what is in season or at the market. This recipe will support about five cups of chopped vegetables. Any more and the batter doesn't hold together well—any less and it's not really vegetable corn bread. I use a variety of chiles and leave the seeds in the rings to give the corn bread some kick, but you could remove them or try chopped zucchini, yellow squash, or eggplant. If you use these more watery vegetables, you should par cook them first to remove some of the moisture (this could be as simple as zapping in the microwave and draining off the excess water). Make sure to seek out whole-grain, not self-rising, cornmeal for the best corn flavor. It is also known as 'nondegerminated.' How's that for a word?"*

Heat the oven to 450°F.

Place the oil in a large cast-iron skillet or ovenproof baking dish and heat in the oven until the oil is piping hot, about 10 minutes. Meanwhile, in a bowl, combine the cornmeal, salt, and baking soda. Add the okra, onion, corn, banana pepper, and chiles and toss to coat. Set aside. In a large measuring cup, combine the buttermilk and egg. Add the wet ingredients to the dry and stir to combine.

Remove the heated skillet from the oven and pour the hot oil into the batter. Stir to combine, and then pour the batter back into the hot skillet. Bake until golden brown, about 35 minutes. Remove to a rack to cool slightly. Using a serrated knife, slice into wedges and serve warm.

UNIVERSAL
MEAT GRINDER

Norman Van Aken
Chef/Owner of Norman's Restaurant
Orlando, Florida

M y universal meat grinder might have been put into a
Goodwill box or tossed aside many years ago but for
some reason, I felt compelled to stow it away and keep
it. It was our Nana's and I think back to late afternoons
in the 1960s when she asked me to set it up by clamping
it to the kitchen counter. The thing was inordinately
heavy for its size! When she used the tool, it showed a
side of her that gave me profound respect—but I was
incapable of giving voice to it back then.

I was just a boy when she came to live with us in Illinois
from her lifelong home in New York City. Her beloved
husband, our grandfather, had passed on. With our
mother away, working at restaurants, Nana became
the new and constant maternal force in our home.

Photograph courtesy of Norman Van Aken

She either made the meals solo or corralled me and my two sisters, Jane and Bet, into helping. When she used the universal grinder, I witnessed an activity of what I heretofore thought of as something masculine. Typically, Nana used her hands *softly* . . . turning the pages of her leather-bound Bible, shaping the dough for her extraordinary scones, or holding one of her favorite opera record album covers pressed to her bosom as she listened, eyes heavenward, in a celestial trance. Yet with this tool she used her lightly freckled Irish hands with gusto, power, and determination. She employed the heavy, iron, mechanistic

> *When my Nana used the tool, it showed a side of her that gave me profound respect.*

device to grind meat and, even more often, cabbages. The squeaking sounds of the coarse green brassica leaves passing through the rudimentary grinder she cranked by its wooden handle shocked me! But the transformation of the once whole leaves to a shredded and cut up slaw emanating from the opposite end fascinated me—despite the funky smell that filled our cozy, lakeside home. She made a simple coleslaw from this ground up matter with a few ingredients . . . the chief among them being *pride*.

NANA'S HAM SALAD

Courtesy of Norman & Janet Van Aken • Makes about 2¼ cups

2 cups baked ham, ground with a grinder or coarsely chopped (we use Kentucky Legend)

¼ cup plus 1 tablespoon mayonnaise (we use Duke's)

2 tablespoons Creole mustard

6 scallions, trimmed of the greens and sliced thin

1 jalapeño, stemmed, seeded and minced

1 tablespoon bottled horseradish

4 tablespoons prepared pickle relish

1 tablespoon fresh lemon juice

Kosher salt and freshly cracked black pepper, to taste

Tabasco or other hot sauce, as desired

"We reached into the family album for this recipe," says Norman Van Aken. *"Our grandmother arrived to our small, nearly out in the country town, not knowing how to drive a car nor the many Midwestern cultural differences we grew up with. But Lord, could she inspire us. This is her trademark ham salad, one my sisters and I loved. That said, Nana did not add jalapeños, but—like families and succeeding generations—we change and, hopefully, flower."*

In a large bowl, combine all of the ingredients. Cover and chill for 2 to 3 hours or overnight. Before serving, let sit at room temperature for about 15 minutes. Serve on crackers or toasts.

Note on the ham: Most folks will likely no longer have a grinder. In that case, pulse the ham briefly in a food processor, being careful not to turn it into paste.

BALLOON WHISK

Dale Levitski
Executive Chef of Sinema and The Hook
Nashville, Tennessee

I'm half Russian, half Swedish—my grandparents came from Sweden—and I grew up on Swedish and German pancakes, which were our family recipes. (My other half of the family was Lithuanian and Russian so we also ate peirogies and potato pies . . . two totally different types of cuisine.)

During Thanksgiving, one of my little projects with Grandma was to help make the whipped cream for her gooseberry pies, which she made every year. Gooseberries are tough to find these days, but my uncle had five gooseberry bushes where we lived in Chicago. They're so tart, you'll suck your face into the back of your head. But Grandma was an amazing baker.

Photograph by MA2LA

In my house, I was the one who always got into trouble. Every year, Grandma would yell at me because I would be helping with the whipped cream, whisking away, and I would always add too much powdered sugar. She would get mad and "tsk tsk" me for over-sweetening the whipped cream.

Fast forward to 2014 and I was moving from Chicago to Nashville to open Sinema. I'd purged just about everything so I needed to restock my kitchen. I found this balloon whisk at Williams-Sonoma. It's just right for so many things. The tines are flexible and there's some heft to it, plus it's larger than most so I find that I can whip cream faster. I'm really picky about whisks. Whenever you order one from a company they're never right; it's one of those things you have to hold in your hand. We do a lot of whisking in our kitchen: every vinaigrette, most of our whipped creams, and every type of batter you can imagine. I now have three of these; two at the restaurant and one at home.

> *Every year, Grandma would yell at me because I would be helping with the whipped cream, whisking away, and I would always add too much powdered sugar.*

DUTCH BABY

Courtesy of Dale Levitski • Serves 4

1 cup milk

4 eggs

3 tablespoons sugar

1 teaspoon vanilla extract

1 tablespoon lemon oil

1 cup flour

2-3 tablespoons butter

Fresh fruit, such as sliced kiwi
and grapefruit

½ cup plain Greek yogurt

Powdered sugar for dusting

This seldom-seen cross between a pancake and a popover is as delicious as it is beautiful. Dusted with powdered sugar, the sweet, crepe-like pastry pairs perfectly with fresh sliced fruit. Heat the oven to 400°F.

In a large bowl, combine the milk, eggs, sugar, vanilla, and lemon oil and whisk together until well combined. Whisk in the flour a little at a time until thoroughly incorporated. Do not overmix. Let the batter rest for 15 minutes.

Place a cast iron skillet in the oven and let heat while batter is resting. Once the skillet is hot, add the butter and let it melt. Add ¾ cup of the batter. Bake for 20 to 25 minutes. Remove when the edges are brown, puffed, and crispy. Repeat with remaining batter.

Top the Dutch baby pancakes with fresh fruit and a dollop of yogurt. Dust with powdered sugar before serving.

PLATING SPOON

Zachary Espinosa
Executive Chef of Harbor House
Milwaukee, Wisconsin

M y plating spoon is the one thing that has been with me since I decided that cooking was my passion. I was working at Bacchus in Milwaukee, which was my first high-level gig—it's still a pretty big-deal restaurant around here—and I needed to outfit my knife kit. I didn't have a lot of money at the time so I went to Goodwill, where I found this really cool spoon. It was pretty well-loved by the time I found it—it didn't have a high luster to it, plus the size is kind of odd because it's too big to be a soup spoon. You wonder sometimes, when you pick up things like this: Did it have a really storied history before me, or was it just in the back of a drawer in someone's house?

Photograph courtesy of Zachary Espinosa

Regardless of its past, the spoon now has its own nickname. When I was working the line at Bacchus, I would use the spoon anytime I was plating something. My station was this stainless steel table, and the spoon would sit in the sanitizer bucket in front of me. Anytime I was up, I would grab the spoon, rinse it, wipe it down, and then bang it as hard as I could against the leg of the table to knock off any last drips of water. That loud clang would let everyone else on the line know that I was about to go up on that dish—like I was a short order cook ringing a bell. Over the years, after banging it over and over again, it developed a bend in the handle, almost like a crook in the neck. That's how it got its name, T.J. Hooker.

You wonder sometimes, when you pick up things like this: Did it have a really storied history before me or was it just in the back of a drawer in someone's house?

It's not a flashy or fancy tool. It's pretty unassuming, in fact. It's just a humble piece of equipment. But it is *always* there for me—for plating, cooking scallops, tasting, everything. In a lot of ways, it speaks to who I am. Call it spoon-y Zen-ism: I'm not super tall. I'm not using crazy gizmos or flashy technology. I keep my head down and I'm always there to do the work. Just like the spoon.

SCALLOPS *with* CORN PUREE & PETITE GREENS SALAD

Courtesy of Zachary Espinosa • Serves 4

Corn Puree:
¼ cup unsalted butter

¼ cup diced shallot

5 cups corn, cut from fresh cobs (about 6 ears)

2 cups heavy cream

Salt and white pepper

Petite Greens Salad:
½ cup extra virgin olive oil

2 tablespoons fresh lemon juice

Salt and black pepper

½ pound petite or baby greens (mache or spring mix)

Scallops:
8 scallops, size U10 or similar

Salt and white pepper

1 tablespoon canola oil

Baby greens and a rich, lightly sweet corn puree are a winning complement to seared and caramelized scallops.

CORN PUREE
In a medium saucepot, melt the butter over medium heat. Add the shallots and sauté until translucent. Add the corn and sweat 2 to 3 minutes. Add the cream and reduce heat to medium low. Cook until cream is reduced by half. Use a blender to puree the corn mixture. Pass it through a fine mesh strainer to remove corn skins. Season with salt and pepper.

PETITE GREENS SALAD
Whisk together the olive oil and lemon juice. Add salt and pepper. Just before serving, toss the greens with the dressing.

SCALLOPS
Pat the scallops dry and lightly season both sides. In a heavy stainless steel sauté pan, heat the oil over medium-high heat. When the oil just starts to smoke, add the scallops one at a time, leaving enough space so that they can be easily flipped. Sauté 2 to 3 minutes or until well browned on one side. Using a large spoon, flip the scallops and repeat the searing process on the second side, cooking 2 to 3 more minutes.

TO SERVE
Place a large spoonful of corn puree on the plate. Top with two scallops and dressed petite greens. Serve at once.

OYSTER KNIFE

Steve McHugh
Chef/Owner of Cured
San Antonio, Texas

M y wife has known me for a really long time—since I was a young, dumb line cook. She's bought me a lot of knives as gifts over the years, so for my fortieth birthday, she gave me this really beautiful oyster knife made by Coastal Custom Knifeworks. The metal of the blade runs all the way through the handle, which is an almost two-toned wood, and it's a thin, strong blade so you know it won't snap. What I love about these knives is that no two are alike.

I grew up in Wisconsin and didn't even know what an oyster was. Then I went to the Culinary Institute of America and for my externship, I decided to go to New Orleans, where I got to work with some of the great old Creole chefs. That's where I learned to shuck, working alongside guys who taught how me to take care of an oyster, to make sure you don't stab the meat, and how to release it properly from the shell. Yes, it's about where oysters come from and how they're handled, but it's also how they're shucked—a shucker can really screw up a good oyster. Like anything, it's a muscle memory.

In my restaurant kitchen, we use the white handled Dexter-Russell knives. (I keep the fancy knife at home.) Usually, I like a blunt tip on my oyster knife because that's how you really work the hinge. That oyster is hanging on for dear life and if you're using something too sharp or thin and you slip off that oyster, it's dangerous. You need something blunt so

> *The metal of the blade runs all the way through the handle, which is an almost two-toned wood, and it's a thin, strong blade so you know it won't snap. What I love about these knives is that no two are alike.*

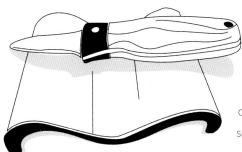

you can find that groove. When you do, it's like finding that perfect combination for a lock and turning the key.

My wife and I live in San Antonio now, but we always have New Orleans inside of us. She's from there and we lived there through Katrina. We went through hell and back in that city, but I will always love it. Whenever I use this oyster knife, it brings me right back home.

MASA FLASH-FRIED OYSTERS & PEARLS

Courtesy of Steve McHugh • Serves 6

Tapioca
4 cups water
1½ cups tapioca pearls

Tangy Herb Mayonnaise
1 egg, boiled for about 9 minutes
 (it should be slightly undercooked)
2 tablespoons chopped onion
1 tablespoon capers
4 anchovies, chopped
1 tablespoon dried mustard
1 tablespoon chopped fresh tarragon
1 tablespoon chopped fresh chives
1 cup mayonnaise
Hot sauce, to taste

Oysters
1 gallon peanut oil
1 egg white, slightly beaten
1 pint freshly shucked oysters
1½ cups masa flour
¾ teaspoon salt, plus more
 for seasoning
1 teaspoon paprika
¾ teaspoon ground black pepper

Cracked open with your favorite oyster knife, this flash-fried recipe offers the lightest of breadings, allowing the oyster to be the rightful star of the dish.

TAPIOCA

In a medium saucepot, bring the water to a boil. Pour in the tapioca and stir frequently with a wooden spoon to keep the pearls from burning. Once the pearls are tender, scoop them out with a slotted spoon and reserve.

TANGY HERB MAYONNAISE

Using a food processor, blend all the ingredients until smooth. Fold into the tapioca pearls and set aside.

OYSTERS

In a two-gallon pot, heat the oil to 360°F. (Use a candy thermometer to gauge your oil temperature.) Meanwhile, place the egg white in a shallow dish and add the oysters. In a medium bowl, mix the flour with the salt, paprika, and black pepper. Remove the oysters from egg white and dredge each oyster through the flour mixture until thoroughly covered. Fry the oysters a few at a time until completely cooked through. Place the oysters on a paper towel-lined plate and season with salt. Serve the oysters over top of the pearls and enjoy.

WOOD-BURNING
INDOOR GRILL

Ford Fry
Executive Chef of The Optimist, King + Duke, Superica, Marcel, El Felix, St. Cecilia, No 246, JCT Kitchen
Atlanta, Georgia

It's every chef's dream to have a sick home kitchen. After dodging requests for interviews in my first home's kitchen for years, I finally had the opportunity to design my own from scratch. My "non-negotiable" was an indoor, wood-burning hearth fitted with a Grillworks grill. I love the experience it creates and, more importantly, the cooking I can do with it.

Cooking over wood fire is such a passion of mine, and this grill is all about flexibility. It features a pulley system, which raises and lowers the cooking surface to achieve low and slow or a full-on quick char. When having friends over for dinner, I always seem to find myself in front of the hearth, roasting everything and anything: porcini mushrooms, whole fish, massive steaks, marinated quail, heritage pork belly, spring ramps, and rustic toast finished with a smear of garlic and summer tomato. During the winter months, as opposed to using a conventional oven for slow-braised dishes like cassoulet, stews, and one-pan quick braises, I can raise the grill grates and cook directly on or by the coals, which adds a perfect amount of light smoke to a dish.

> *I love the experience it creates and, more importantly, the cooking I can do with it.*

I often imagine how it used to be when everything was cooked over burning wood—people of that age never knew they had it so good! Imagine duck legs, salt-cured and slow-simmered in their own fat while taking on the flavors of the type of wood being used. Now imagine that slightly smoky, salty duck, slow cooking with winter beans and cured sausage in duck broth! It's cooking with love, passion, and patience that totally excites me. I know there are other ways to achieve this excitement—but for me, this is simply the best.

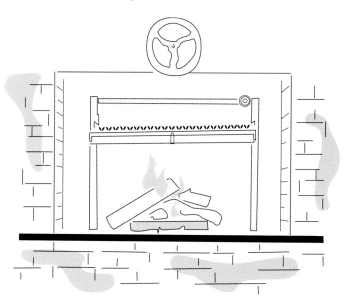

PAN CON TOMATE

Courtesy of Ford Fry • Serves 6

Six 1-inch slices of crusty rustic bread

½ cup extra virgin olive oil

Maldon sea salt to taste

1 fresh garlic clove

2 very ripe local tomatoes, cut in half crosswise

When you start with good tomatoes and good bread, little else is needed. Here, the wood-fired grill lends just enough flavor and toasts the bread, making it the perfect accompaniment for freshly cut tomatoes.

Heat a wood-burning grill to medium high heat (or heat an oven to 450°F). Brush the bread slices generously with olive oil. Season to taste with Maldon salt. Grill (or oven toast) the bread slices until the edges toast up, about 1 to 2 minutes (the centers should be medium toasted and still chewy). Softly rub the garlic clove across the toast. Then, rub the super-ripe tomato over the toast, somewhat smashing the tomato. Serve warm.

WOODEN SPOON

Kevin Gillespie
Chef and Owner of Gunshow and Revival
Atlanta, Georgia

About 13 years ago, I found this wooden spoon in the tool bin at the Ritz-Carlton Atlanta where I worked at the time. It didn't belong to anybody—it sort of belonged to the universe. It had a Culinary Institute of America logo on the handle, so I just assumed it had once been issued in the tool kit there. At the time, it was the one spoon that was used whenever someone was making risotto. The top had been whittled down so that it was almost flat, which made it perfect for stirring a big batch.

When I was there, it would get passed down the line so that whoever was on that station inherited the spoon. I now jokingly refer to it as Arthur and his sword—I just sort of pulled it from the bin one day

Photograph by Andrew Thomas Lee

and suddenly it was mine. The reason I still have it is because I happened to be the last person using it when a new chef came in and the risotto went off the menu—the spoon became superfluous. Coincidentally, I decided to leave around the same time and I thought to myself, "I'll just return the spoon to where I found it." But the rest of the kitchen was like,No man, that's yours, just take it with you." I've had it ever since.

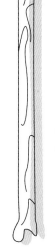

It probably used to be about 15 inches long or so, but it's been beat to hell and back. The bowl is more like a flat shovel and it's been burned, broken, and whittled down so much that it's more like a spatula than a spoon now. I still use it anytime I'm making risotto or anything where I'm trying to scrape the bottom of the pan, or getting around the edges—a regular wooden spoon is too round. So this spoon is perfect.

> *I still use it anytime I'm making risotto or anything where I'm trying to scrape the bottom of the pan, or getting around the edges—a regular wooden spoon is too round. So this spoon is perfect.*

I keep it in the tool bin at Gunshow now, but it doesn't seem to make it out very frequently. Inevitably, someone new will come in and ask what it is. The response is usually, "Oh, that's just Kevin's spoon." And the new person will say, "I didn't know Kevin went to the CIA." It's just this ongoing joke. And what's even better is that I've met and worked with so many people who did go to the CIA and not one of them remembers a spoon like this being in their toolkit. It's like its provenance is unknown—and yet I cannot bear to part with it.

PORK SKIN RISOTTO

Courtesy of Kevin Gillespie • Serves 4

1 cup pancetta diced small

1 baseball size onion diced small

1 cup farro piccolo

1 quart chicken stock

2 cloves garlic, finely minced

2 tablespoons unsalted butter

1 cup freshly fried pork rinds, finely
  ground in food processor

Salt and pepper to taste

Juice of 2 lemons

Extra virgin olive oil, for garnish

Starting with good pancetta and being sure to scrape up all the browned bits from the bottom of the pan provides the flavor for this savory risotto. The addition of pork rinds at the end is a winning and welcome twist.

In a heavy-bottomed pan, render the pancetta over medium-low heat. Don't allow it to get too crispy; cook until just light golden brown. Add the onion. Cook until light golden brown. Add the farro and stir really well so all the grains become covered in fat. Cook for about 1 minute, stirring constantly so the farro doesn't burn. Increase heat to medium-high and add about ½ cup chicken stock, allowing it to soak into the grains; continue stirring. Add more stock, ½ cup at a time, whenever the liquid has absorbed. (Allow liquid to simmer but not boil.) Continue adding stock until the farro becomes tender enough to chew, about 25 to 30 minutes. Remove from the heat. Add 2 more tablespoons of chicken stock plus the garlic, butter, and pork rinds. Stir to combine until slightly thickened. Season to taste with salt, pepper, and lemon juice. Place in bowls and garnish with olive oil.

ROLLING PIN

Natalie Chanin
Designer/Chef/Owner of Alabama Chanin
Florence, Alabama

Biscuit making holds a certain status in Southern culture—both in culinary and neighborhood circles. Almost everyone who makes biscuits has a steadfast technique or ingredient they use, though not everyone is keen on sharing those tips and tricks. I believe in both the concept of open sourcing and the healing power of biscuits, so my recipes are happily shared.

Through a strange series of twists and turns, biscuits have come to define much of my cooking life. I've made pans and pans and pans of biscuits, delved into the difference between this flour and that, and fed multitudes with this lowly (yet oh-so-elevated) bread. For a dish so closely associated with Southern cooking, I have spent almost as much time making

biscuits *outside* of the South as I have in the South. My nickname, Alabama, was coined when a group of friends in Venezuela couldn't pronounce the word "biscuit" and referred to my round morning bread as "pan de Alabama," and, consequently, me as "Alabama."

For 30 years, the same rolling pin—given to me by my mother when I moved away from home at 18—has traveled the world with me: Alabama to Tennessee to North Carolina to New York City to Europe, around the world and back again (a couple of times). I don't know where my mother got this rolling pin and there isn't anything spectacular about it—just no-frills practicality. It isn't especially large or small. The

> *I believe in both the concept of open sourcing and the healing power of biscuits, so my recipes are happily shared.*

wood doesn't have a beautiful grain or patterning and the handles aren't really useful—and who needs them, anyway? But it's mine and has made thousands of biscuit brigades—twelve little round soldiers at a time—that have fed many hungry mouths, with many more to come. I guess it is just a reminder that tools needn't be extravagant when you are cooking with great intention.

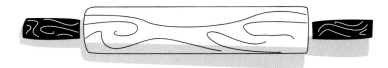

NATALIE'S BISCUIT RECIPE

Courtesy of Natalie Chanin • Makes about one dozen biscuits

2 cups all-purpose flour, plus 1 cup
    for rolling out dough

2 teaspoons baking powder (use
    homemade if you can)

1 teaspoon salt

1 stick plus 2 tablespoons unsalted
    butter (stick cut into cubes and
    chilled; tablespoons melted)

¾ cup whole milk or half-and-half

This light biscuit goes well with a wide array of meals, or can be paired with a simple pat of butter as treat all by itself.

Heat the oven to 425°F. In a large bowl, combine 2 cups of flour with the baking powder and salt and mix thoroughly (or sift together). Using a pastry blender or 2 knives, cut cubed butter into mixture until it resembles coarse meal. Stir in milk until a soft dough forms. Turn the dough out onto a lightly floured surface and knead 2 or 3 times, until it just comes together. Then use a lightly floured rolling pin to roll out dough ¼ inch thick. Fold dough in half and roll out to ¼ inch thick again to laminate (or flatten) butter into layers. Repeat several times, until the butter is all flattened and the dough is springy to the touch. Finish by rolling out dough ½ inch thick.

Using a lightly floured 2¼-inch round cutter, stamp out biscuits as close together as possible. Pat the dough scraps together, laminate the dough together again, and cut more biscuits. Transfer the biscuits to a large baking sheet lined with parchment paper, making sure that the sides of the biscuits are touching to get additional rise from your dough. Bake about 10 minutes, or until the biscuits have risen and the tops are golden brown. (If your oven bakes unevenly, rotate the pan at 5 minutes.) Remove pan from oven and turn it off. Brush biscuits with melted butter, then return to cooling oven to sit for several minutes. Remove from oven and serve hot.

SHARKSKIN
WASABI GRATER

Ken Oringer
Executive Chef of Clio, Uni, Toro, Coppa, and Earth
Boston, Massachusetts

Before my first trip to Japan, I'd never heard of cooking with fresh wasabi. It was the year 2000 when this notion changed after I stumbled across a sharkskin wasabi grater in a shop outside Tokyo's famous Tsukiji Fish Market. Flash forward 15 years, and I now use this tool at home, at my restaurants, and even give them as gifts all the time. People aren't used to seeing fresh wasabi, and if they are, then they're not used to seeing it grated like this. You can throw this grater in your knife kit and it's fantastic for sashimi on the go. When I'm in Maine, I'll serve lobster sashimi with fresh wasabi; when I'm down South, I'll use it for oysters with fresh wasabi and a bit of lemon. It's really fun—I take it everywhere.

Photograph this page by Noah Fecks. Opposite: istock.com/JindiRamisa

LIVE SEA URCHIN *with* FRESH GRATED WASABI, LEMON & PICKLED MUSTARD SEEDS

Courtesy of Ken Oringer • Serves 2

1 cup rice wine vinegar

1 teaspoon salt (plus extra for garnish)

½ cup sugar

2 tablespoons yellow mustard seeds

2 live sea urchins (1 per person)

Juice from 1 lemon

1 teaspoon soy sauce

Fresh wasabi (to taste)

Uni, the edible part of a live sea urchin, is often found in sushi dishes but stands on its own when paired with traditional Asian flavors.

THE DAY BEFORE

In a medium-sized pan, combine the rice wine vinegar, salt, and sugar and bring to a boil. Pour into a jar, add mustard seeds, and let seeds soak overnight.

THE DAY OF

Take live urchin and cut a wide circle through the mouth using an urchin knife or two spoons. Turn the urchin over and drain the contents into a bowl. Discard the cut-out opening of the sea urchin as well as all of the liquid contents. Using a small spoon, scoop out the orange roe, or uni, from the shell (depending on the size, it might be 2 to 6 scoops). Place uni in an ice bath to rinse off and remove any dark matter.

TO SERVE

Place cleaned uni in two small serving dishes. Drizzle with lemon juice and soy sauce. Garnish with pickled mustard seeds. Sprinkle with sea salt and grate fresh wasabi over the top before serving.

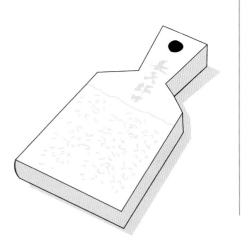

GRANDFATHER'S
SKILLET

Linton Hopkins

Executive Chef of Restaurant Eugene, Holeman and Finch Public House, Linton's in the Garden, H&F Burger, and Hop's Chicken
Atlanta, Georgia

When my grandfather, Eugene Holeman, after whom my wife Gina and I named our flagship restaurant, passed away I received two major things from him: his beloved Griswold cast iron skillet and a beaten biscuit roller. The skillet, made in Erie, Pennsylvania, has become my favorite piece of culinary equipment. It's a round skillet with minimal edges, making it more like a shallow griddle, and the Griswold trademark cross is imprinted on the back. I love all shapes and sizes of cast iron skillets, but this was the first one that I had seen without deep sides. I have fond memories of my grandfather using it to make my sister and me pancakes when we were children. I now use it all the time to make my own kids pancakes for breakfast and Johnny-Cakes at dinner; I even use it as a meat press. I love it. It's one of those totems that whenever I bring it out, I think of him.

JOHNNY-CAKES

Courtesy of Linton Hopkins • Makes about 10 to 12 cakes

⅔ cup all-purpose flour
⅔ cup cornmeal
1 teaspoon baking soda
1 teaspoon kosher salt
¾ cup buttermilk
½ cup whole milk
2 whole eggs
3-4 tablespoons butter

Johnny-cakes may be the quintessential dish to prepare in your favorite iron skillet. This recipe mixes equal parts of flour and meal for a flexible dinnertime stand-by.

In a large mixing bowl, combine the dry ingredients. In a medium-sized mixing bowl, whisk together the buttermilk, milk, and eggs. Pour the wet ingredients into the dry ingredients and whisk until just combined. Heat a cast iron skillet until hot. Add a tablespoon of butter and cook until it froths. Add 2 tablespoons of batter per Johnny-Cake and cook until the batter bubbles in the center and the edges are brown and crispy, about 1½ to 2 minutes. Flip, and cook until firm and the second side is browned, about 1½ minutes. Continue cooking cakes, adding more butter as needed. Serve warm.

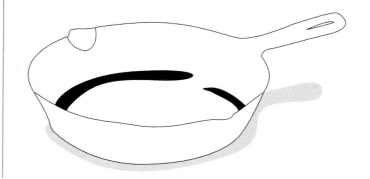

MORTAR & PESTLE

Alon Shaya

Executive Chef of Shaya; Executive Chef and Partner of Domenica and Pizza Domenica

New Orleans, Louisiana

There was a time in the late 1800s when my great grandmother, Devora, would grind spices and crush garlic using a thick, solid brass mortar and pestle. She kept it on the top shelf of her small apartment in Bulgaria and would pull it down at times to cook with my young grandmother, Matilda, who I call "Savta." I inherited my grandmother's passion for cooking and attribute my instincts in the kitchen and with my palate to her. Savta escaped Bulgaria during World War II to travel to a newly born Israel. Whatever essentials she had to pack for the trip made way for this five-pound tool. It must have meant a lot to her to be added to the packing list. She used it in Israel to cook for my mother, Alisa, and my Aunt Debbie,

Photography by Marianna Massey

Devora's namesake. The sounds of the grinding process were heard from the next room when she used it—my mom and Debbie distinctly recall its bell-like sound. To them, that sound signified dinner would be served shortly.

After my grandfather's passing, Savta began to share some of the family heirlooms with my mom and Aunt Debbie. By that time I had already graduated from culinary school and was cooking in St. Louis. My Savta knew I wanted to be a chef, though I'm not sure she ever realized the influence she would have on my life. She asked my mother to bring the mortar and pestle to me so I could

After a close call in customs at the airport in Tel Aviv, in which my mom had to scold a young Israeli soldier for showing suspicion—think "mortar" and "pistol"—the treasure was mine.

continue to use it. After a close call in customs at the airport in Tel Aviv, in which my mom had to scold a young Israeli soldier for showing suspicion— think "mortar" and "pistol"—the treasure was mine. I use it now to grind spices, but really I like to make it ring and think of my Savta.

MOROCCAN CARROT SALAD

Courtesy of Alon Shaya • Serves 4 to 6

8 cups baby heirloom carrots

½ cup canola oil

2 tablespoons Harissa (recipe follows)

¼ cup apple cider vinegar

1¼ tablespoons kosher salt

1 tablespoon sugar

1 teaspoon freshly grated orange zest

½ teaspoon cumin seeds, toasted and ground fine

¾ teaspoon caraway seeds, toasted and ground fine

¾ teaspoon amba, dry powder

¼ cup plus 3 tablespoons olive oil

1 cup thinly sliced onions

Small fresh mint leaves

Harissa
Makes about ½ cup

2 dried guajillo chiles

15 dried chile de árbol

1 dried ancho chile

1½ teaspoons whole coriander

1 tablespoon cumin seeds

1½ teaspoons smoked paprika

1½ tablespoons kosher salt

2 garlic cloves

1 tablespoon white wine vinegar

1 teaspoon tomato paste

1½ tablespoons fresh lemon juice

½ cup olive oil

Heirloom carrots dressed in harissa made from freshly ground herbs and spices create a dish as tasty as it is simple.

Heat oven to 325°F. Wash the baby carrots and trim off the tops leaving ¼-inch of stalk. Toss carrots with canola oil and place on a baking sheet. Roast the carrots for 10 to 15 minutes just until they soften but are not cooked all the way through.

Meanwhile, in a large bowl, whisk together the harissa, vinegar, salt, sugar, orange zest, cumin, caraway, and amba powder. Slowly whisk in the olive oil. Remove the carrots from the oven and, while still warm, toss them with the onions and dress with the vinaigrette. Garnish with small mint leaves.

HARISSA

Bring two quarts of water to a boil. Remove the stems from dried chiles and place in a large bowl. Pour boiling water over chiles and let sit until are fully rehydrated, approximately 1 hour. Drain and remove skins and seeds. In a small sauté pan, toast coriander and cumin seeds over high heat for 2 minutes until fragrant. Using a mortar and pestle, finely crush the toasted coriander and cumin with the smoked paprika and salt. Add the garlic cloves and vinegar and continue grinding together. Once a paste is created, add the chiles to the mortar and pestle and incorporate into the spice mixture.

In a clean bowl, fold the spice and pepper mixture into the tomato paste. Add the lemon juice and olive oil and continue folding together until well combined.

COCONUT
BENCH SCRAPER

Bruce Sherman
Executive Chef of North Pond
Chicago, Illinois

My wife and I lived in Dehli, India, for almost four years in the '90s—her job took us there and I was the trailing spouse, which I highly recommend to anyone who gets the opportunity. While we were there, I spent a lot of time in Kerala, a state down towards the south, studying the food, customs, and spices. Of all the regions and states in India, of which there are many, Kerala really grabbed me. I think it was a byproduct not only of the nature of the curries and the richness of the coconut milk that I found in so much of the food, but also the richness and the intensity of the people.

I discovered this coconut bench scraper in a shop in the historic part of Kochi. It was just so beautiful and also practical. Scrapers are a relic of both a different time as well as the culture there. Much of the food is steeped in coconut—it's much more closely related to the foods of Thailand or Malaysia or Sri Lanka than most people think. It's humid and it's on the coast—and many of the spices that we use here in the West are grown there. It's also rife with coconut palms, so naturally the coconut is a revered icon of the area.

The one I have has to be about 100 years old. It's made from a fruitwood tree, and nowadays they don't allow those trees to get very old. You can see the grain in the wood on it. Typically, in an Indian home, something like this would be used by servants to grate coconuts but one this aesthetically beautiful is very rare. To use it, you set it at an angle and, using half a coconut at a time, you rotate the fruit 180 degrees back and forth

> *For special occasions, we might use freshly grated coconut or coconut milk—but it's hard to use something like this tool when working on that scale. Instead, I keep this one prominently displayed inside my kitchen at home.*

and also 360 degrees around to scrape out the meat, which falls into the bowl. You then blend the meat with water to make coconut milk.

After cooking in India for so many years, I still put variations of those dishes on my menu from time to time. For special occasions, we might use freshly grated coconut or coconut milk—but it's hard to use something like this tool when working on that scale. Instead, I keep this one prominently displayed inside my kitchen at home.

CASHEW *or* PEANUT CURRY

Courtesy of Bruce Sherman • Serves 4

¼ cup whole coriander seeds

½ stick cinnamon

1 teaspoon fennel seeds

¼ teaspoon turmeric

½ teaspoon red chile flakes

1 teaspoon black peppercorns

4 whole cloves

1 teaspoon salt

2 tablespoons coconut oil

1 medium onion, peeled and finely sliced

3 ounces fresh ginger, peeled and finely julienned

1 fresh jalapeño, thinly sliced

8 ounces raw cashews or peanuts

1 cup water or vegetable stock

1 can (13.5-ounce) coconut milk, refrigerated, with "cream" separated from milk (or, if using fresh coconut, 2 cups coconut water from 2nd extract and ½ cup coconut cream from 1st extract)

12-16 ounces cooked chicken breast, cut into pieces (or cooked shrimp)

Prepared rice or grain of choice

Toasted spices lend flavor to this spicy nut curry, which works nicely with either chicken or shrimp.

Place the coriander, cinnamon, fennel, turmeric, chile flakes, peppercorns, cloves, and salt in a spice or coffee grinder and grind to a powder. Reserve.

In a large heavy-bottomed pot, heat the coconut oil over medium heat. Add the onion, ginger, and jalapeño. Stir constantly to soften, about 4 minutes. Add the ground spice mixture and toast, stirring constantly for 1 minute, scraping the bottom to prevent sticking. Add the nuts, stock, and coconut milk or water (from bottom of separated can or fresh). Bring to a boil and then cover; lower the heat and let simmer until the nuts soften, about 1 to 1¼ hours.

Add the chicken or shrimp and gently return to a boil. Finish by stirring in reserved coconut "cream" and seasoning to taste. Serve with rice or other grain.

FLUTED
PARISIAN SCOOPS

Timothy Hollingsworth
Executive Chef of Otium LA
Los Angeles, California

I t was my first time traveling to France—my first time overseas, actually. It was 2004, and I had been working in French kitchens for my entire life at this point. Finally, I had gotten the chance to explore the country that had inspired so many years of cooking and had been my motivation throughout the long hours on the line. I had spent years at The French Laundry, and was about to go to New York to open up Per Se, but first I flew to France to stage at the Michelin-starred Michel Rostang and the famed Lucas Carton.

I was walking through a flea market and came across these awesome antique fluted scoops. They were just so original that I had to buy them. They have this great rustic quality to them, and give the food an interesting aesthetic. I just happened upon these unique pieces at a street market, and was able to bring home something that you cannot find anymore—nobody has these shapes and sizes.

The fluted scoops remind of the moment in my life when my career really began to take off. I used them in many special VIP dishes at The French Laundry and they have become an important part of my kit.

I was walking through a flea market and came across these awesome antique fluted scoops. They were just so original that I had to buy them.

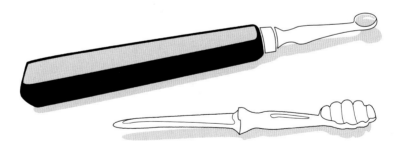

HAMACHI TARTARE *with* SWEET & SOUR TOMATOES

Courtesy of Timothy Hollingsworth • Serves 4

Tartare
1 pound fresh hamachi
Zest of 1 lime
2 tablespoons Maldon sea salt
6-8 sheets of nori, shredded into
 fine strips

Sweet and Sour Tomatoes
½ cup Sweet 100 tomatoes
½ cup Sungold tomatoes
½ cup sugar
½ cup water
¼ cup Champagne vinegar

To Serve
1 avocado, preferably Haas
Sliced fresh ginger

Tomatoes and scoops of molded avocado accompany fresh hamachi, or yellowtail, a white, mellow fish that is also a sushi favorite.

TARTARE
Slice the hamachi into thin pieces. In a small bowl, mix together the lime zest and Maldon salt. Place hamachi in a shallow dish and season both sides with lime/salt mixture. Cover loosely and refrigerate; cure for about 6 hours. When you're ready to serve, dice the hamachi into 1-inch pieces. Place nori shreds in a shallow bowl and dip hamachi pieces into the nori. Set aside.

SWEET AND SOUR TOMATOES
Cut Sweet 100s and Sungold tomatoes in half. Combine sugar, water, and vinegar and place tomatoes in brine. Let sit for 5 to 10 minutes.

TO SERVE
Cut the avocado in half and remove the pit. Using a fluted Parisian scoop, scoop out small pieces of avocado. Arrange the hamachi, avocado, marinated tomatoes, and ginger on a plate and serve.

MINI
MEAT FORK

Slade Rushing
Executive Chef of Brennan's Restaurant
New Orleans, Louisiana

One of the most important things about working in a professional kitchen is having the right tools within reach at all times. Whether cooking, plating, or simply transporting food, having the right tools for the job can make you or break you in this high-pressure environment. The right tool can make tasks look and feel effortless, giving you the aura of a culinary superhero, while the wrong tool can simply ruin hours of long, hard work and be a very expensive mistake. My favorite tool to have in my arsenal is the F. Dick mini meat fork.

While I was working at New York's Fleur de Sel, which closed in 2009, this was a non negotiable tool to have in your spoon bain at all times.

Photograph by Chris Granger

Chef Cyril Renaud hated tongs, and this was his favorite tool since it could be used either for turning or checking for doneness in fish and other foods. I believe this tool could be traced to his days in David Bouley's kitchen and could have even been a favorite of David's as well.

My favorite thing about the mini meat fork is those times when you're searing proteins such as scallops—you can gently turn the scallops without destroying them like you might with tongs. The fork can also come in handy when checking braised dishes for doneness. Another great method for this tool is when plating pasta such as fresh fettuccine. It allows you to twist it

My favorite thing about the mini meat fork is those times when you're searing proteins such as scallops—you can gently turn the scallops without destroying them like you might with tongs.

around in a tight roll before you lay the pasta into a bowl. The fork I use now is made by F. Dick; I picked it up at kitchen supplier JB Prince when I was living in New York. I still use it for everything—I'm never without it.

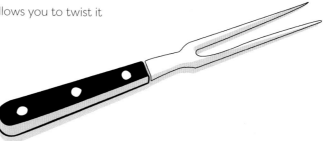

FETTUCCINE *with* CRUSHED TOMATO, BLUE CRAB & DILL

Courtesy of Slade Rushing • Serves 4

1 pound fettuccine, preferably fresh

½ cup dry white wine

2 ounces Crushed Tomato Condiment
  (recipe follows)

4 ounces unsalted butter

8 ounces jumbo lump blue crabmeat

1 tablespoon chopped fresh dill

1 lemon, juiced and zested

Salt and pepper, to taste

Crushed Tomato Condiment
Makes about 1¼ cups

1 pint cherry tomatoes

1 tablespoon chopped garlic

1 tablespoon chopped shallots

2 cups extra virgin olive oil

2 sprigs thyme

¼ teaspoon salt

¼ teaspoon chile flakes

The sharp taste of dill complements crushed tomato and blue crab folded into fettuccine for a quick and easy meal.

Cook the fettuccine in a pot of boiling water until al dente. Meanwhile, using a large sauté pan, bring the wine and Crushed Tomato Condiment to a simmer. Slowly whisk in the butter until sauce is formed. Add the crab, dill, and cooked pasta to the sauce, toss well, then season with salt, pepper, and lemon juice to taste. Twist the pasta using a meat fork until four equal size portions are formed, then plate them all individually. Spoon the pan sauce over the pasta and add more fresh dill if desired. Garnish with the lemon zest.

CRUSHED TOMATO CONDIMENT

Combine all the ingredients in a medium saucepan and bring to a slow simmer over medium-low heat. Let simmer for 20 minutes. Drain off excess oil, remove the thyme, and crush the tomatoes lightly with a fork. Reserve 2 ounces for this dish and save the rest for another use.

HAND-CRANK
CHEESE GRATER

Michael Scelfo
Chef and Owner, Alden & Harlow
Cambridge, Massachusetts

This old cheese grater belonged to my grandmother and grandfather on my dad's side, Josephine and Joseph. Both sides of my family grew up around the block from each other—my mom and dad started dating when they were 11 years old and have been together ever since. It was very typical of that era and that part of Long Island, New York, which was also very Italian American. The cheese grater sat in my grandparents' kitchen in New York and later in Virginia, where they retired. I came across it in my aunt's garage after my grandfather passed away and it's been on the counter in my own kitchen ever since. We might not have a lot of photos of my grandparents around the house, but having this in the kitchen and walking by it a hundred times a day is really meaningful to me.

It has to be 60 years old at this point—it was once fire engine red, but it's so beat up and weathered now. They used it daily because that's how everyone ate, all the time. My grandparents loved to cook together—side-by-side in the kitchen all day long—and there was always a huge table set. They lived for their family and food was everything—sauce, especially, was king. But there were also meatballs and sausage, huge pots with pasta, cutlets and huge salads, plus eggplant parm, and linguine with clam sauce. This was a Pecorino Romano family—we were mostly Sicilian, so that sharp, sheep's milk cheese was in everything. I bet that grater only ever saw Pecorino while my

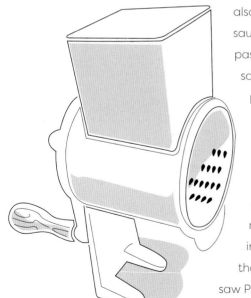

> *This was a Pecorino Romano family—we were mostly Sicilian, so that sharp, sheep's milk cheese was in everything. I bet that grater only ever saw Pecorino while my grandparents were alive.*

grandparents were alive. To me, some dishes don't taste right unless they have that acidity of Pecorino.

I still love to cook like they did, and will cook those dishes every chance I get, especially at the holidays. And I always use the grater, mostly for the nostalgia of it. It's an old piece now—the handle comes off easily and it's finicky. The teeth are so ground down that you have to use a little pressure to hold the cheese down—it almost becomes a two-man job. You can tell it wants to fall apart, but we're not going to let it.

GRANDMA'S MANICOTTI

Courtesy of Michael Scelfo • Makes 24 manicotti

Sauce

Two 28-ounce cans chunky "kitchen-ready" tomatoes, preferably Pastene

Water

½ cup extra virgin olive oil

8 to 10 cloves garlic, finely chopped

One 6-ounce can tomato paste, preferably Contadina

1 teaspoon red pepper flakes

1 tablespoon sugar

24 fresh basil leaves, roughly chopped, divided

Kosher salt and freshly ground pepper

Shells

2 cups all-purpose flour

2 cups water

2 eggs

Pinch of salt

Olive oil

Freshly grated ricotta, mozzarella, and Pecorino lend a complex combination of flavors in what may be the epitome of comfort food.

SAUCE

Place tomatoes in a large bowl. Fill one of the empty cans with water and pour into the other empty can to rinse out all of the excess tomato sauce and add to tomatoes. Stir to combine.

In a Dutch oven or heavy-bottomed pot, heat the olive oil over medium-low heat. Add the garlic and cook until fragrant, about 30 seconds. Add the tomato paste, red pepper flakes, sugar, and half of the chopped basil leaves. Stir to combine and cook, stirring occasionally, until mixture is deeply caramelized, about 30 minutes. Add the tomato mixture and season with salt and pepper. Bring to a simmer, cover and let simmer for 1 hour. Uncover and continue simmering for 1 more hour. Fold in the remaining basil leaves and remove from the heat. Set aside. (This can be made a day ahead and refrigerated. Let sit at room temperature for 30 minutes before assembling the dish.)

SHELLS

Combine flour, water, egg, and salt in a large bowl and whisk together until smooth. Heat a 6-inch cast-iron skillet over high

(continued on next page)

GRANDMA'S MANICOTTI *(continued)*

Filling and Assembly

16 ounces whole milk ricotta

1½ cups shredded or diced whole
  milk mozzarella

1½ cups Pecorino, grated, plus more
  for topping

4 eggs

¼ cup fresh flat-leaf parsley, chopped

Kosher salt and freshly ground
  black pepper

heat. Add enough oil to barely coat the pan and swirl. Add 2 tablespoons of batter and swirl to create a flat disk. Cook for 30 seconds, then flip and cook for another 30 seconds. Remove pasta and repeat until batter is gone, adding a small amount of olive oil before making each shell. (Should make about 24 shells.) Set aside. (These can be made a day ahead and refrigerated.)

FILLING AND ASSEMBLY

In a large bowl, combine the ricotta, mozzarella, Pecorino, eggs, and parsley. Season with salt and pepper to taste.

Heat the oven to 350°F.

To assemble: Ladle a small amount of sauce on the bottom of a rimmed, nonstick baking sheet. Lay one sheet of pasta on a flat surface and spread 2 tablespoons of cheese filling in the center of the sheet. Roll the pasta into a tubular shell. Place the shell on the baking sheet. Continue with the remaining shells, filling the baking sheet. Ladle the remaining tomato sauce over the shells and finish with a healthy sprinkle of Pecorino. Bake for 40 minutes or until the shells are heated through and sauce is bubbling.

WOODEN SPOON

David Guas
Host of Travel Channel's *American Grilled*; Chef and
Owner of Bayou Bakery, Coffee Bar & Eatery
Arlington, Virginia

G rowing up, I had no boundaries. I would tell lies to
get out of trouble, pick fights with my sister, and
just cause havoc wherever—and whenever—I could
get away with it . . . or thought I could. When my mom
and dad had had enough of me for the moment, they
would send me to Aunt Boo's in Abbeville, Louisiana,
three hours west of New Orleans. As Aunt Boo saw it,
it would be good, clean, wholesome fun (and help me
gain back my righteousness) to cook with her. And it all
started with a roux and a wooden spoon. To this day,
inside a ceramic bucket of varied utensils next to my
stove, I still have the wooden spoon she gave me. I've
had it for 30 years—the burned scars and worn sides
prove its worth.

Today, Aunt Boo could out-cook some of the best chefs across the South. She still kicks my butt in the kitchen—and I've been a trained chef for 18 years. In her kitchen, there's nothing fancy on display, like copper pots or $200 knives that are sold in special cases. Instead, there are a few blackened cast iron skillets, functional pots and pans for her gumbos and étouffée, and a well-worn oven.

The customary pose for Aunt Boo is to be standing with a wooden spoon in one hand and a cold beer in the other, stirring up a pot of something that smells strongly of the soulful South. One bite or slurp off her wooden spoon and it confirms that I was born in the right state: Louisiana. Only while I was standing beside

As Aunt Boo saw it, it would be good, clean, wholesome fun (and help me gain back my righteousness) to cook with her. And it all started with a roux and a wooden spoon.

her at the stove growing up as a young teen, did I feel completely comfortable, like I'd found a place of order and rules that would not, and could not, be broken under any circumstances. It was my time in Aunt Boo's kitchen that laid the foundation for my future— for becoming a respectful and purposeful chef in my own kitchen.

BUTTERMILK BISCUITS & CRAWFISH GRAVY

Courtesy of David Guas • Serves 4

Biscuits

2¼ cups all-purpose flour, preferably White Lily (not self-rising)

2 tablespoons baking powder

¾ teaspoon kosher salt

1 cup buttermilk

1 stick unsalted butter, cold, cut into small bits, plus 2 tablespoons, melted

Served over biscuits for brunch or a decadent breakfast, this spicy crawfish gravy gets a kick of umami from a healthy dose of Worchestershire sauce.

BISCUITS

Heat the oven to 400°F. Line a baking sheet with parchment paper and set aside. Place 2 cups of flour, baking powder, and salt in a food processor and pulse to combine. Add the stick of butter and process for 10 one-second pulses until the pieces of butter are no larger than small peas. Transfer to a large bowl and add ¾ cup of the buttermilk, incorporating it into the dry ingredients by mixing with your hands and moving in circular motions. Add just enough buttermilk to form a dough.

Dust a work surface with the remaining flour and place the dough on top. With a rolling pin, roll it out to 1-inch thickness. Using a 2¼-inch round biscuit cutter, punch out as many biscuits as you can and place them on the parchment lined baking sheet. Gently bring the dough scraps together and press to a 1-inch thickness. Punch out a few more biscuits, place them on the baking sheet, and discard scraps.

Brush the tops of the biscuits with the remaining buttermilk and bake until golden brown, 20 to 25 minutes. Remove from oven and brush with the melted butter.

(continued on next page)

BUTTERMILK BISCUITS & CRAWFISH GRAVY *(continued)*

Crawfish Gravy:

¼ cup cooking oil (grapeseed or canola oil/olive oil blend)

1 cup small diced sweet onions

⅓ cup small diced green bell pepper

⅓ cup small diced celery

1 teaspoon minced garlic

1 pound crawfish tail meat, fresh or thawed if frozen

2 tablespoons Worcestershire sauce

½ teaspoon cayenne pepper

½ teaspoon ground black pepper

1 tablespoon kosher salt

¾ cup all-purpose flour

1 quart whole milk

3 scallions, thinly sliced on the bias

CRAWFISH GRAVY

In a large sauté pan, heat the oil over medium-high for 1 minute. Add the onions, bell peppers, and celery and cook for 5 minutes. Add the garlic and continue to cook for 5 more minutes. Add the crawfish meat and sauté for 5 minutes. Add the Worcestershire sauce, cayenne, black pepper, and salt. Using a wooden spoon, stir in the flour. Cook, stirring occasionally for 5 minutes. Add the milk, one cup at a time, stirring after each addition. Lower heat to medium low and gently simmer for 5 minutes. Adjust seasonings to taste.

TO SERVE

Split a biscuit in half and place both pieces in a bowl. Using a 2-ounce ladle, portion the gravy over the biscuit. Garnish with the scallions.

MICROPLANE

Sean Brasel
Executive Chef of Meat Market
Miami, Florida

About 15 or 20 years ago, I was at an event doing a demonstration—I honestly can't remember where I was or what I was about to prepare—and there was a pastry chef doing a demo right before me. I remember this so clearly: He finished the dessert and pulled out this teeny little metal grating tool and he started grating cinnamon and nutmeg over the dessert. I'd never seen a Microplane before, and it completely stopped me in my tracks. I thought I knew everything, but this just left me floored. Everything left my mind except: "I have to find one of those tools."

Microplanes weren't widely available then, so I searched hardware stores and kitchen supply houses until I finally found one on the Internet. This was before they had rubber handles, even. It's one of the very best ways to get a truly natural flavor from an ingredient—just think about the difference between cinnamon you grate fresh over a Microplane versus something that comes out of a jar.

I'd say thirty percent of the ingredients in our kitchen at Meat Market go over a Microplane now. Essentially, any product that is really hard, or you can make really hard, can be made into a microfine powder. We use it for lemons, limes, and Parmesan, of course, but I love using it for horseradish root and even foie gras, which we freeze using liquid nitrogen before grating. Chorizo, leftover cookies, garlic—really, you can use it with anything. (But I'm still trying to figure out how to grate black peppercorns.)

I'd never seen a Microplane before, and it completely stopped me in my tracks. I thought I knew everything, but this just left me floored.

Chefs like their knives sharp and I feel the same way about my Microplane—I actually go through one every two months or so, because I want them really, really sharp. I have a couple lined up, and I'll switch out the colors every time. I have a brand new purple one in my knife kit right now, and it will come with me everywhere I go.

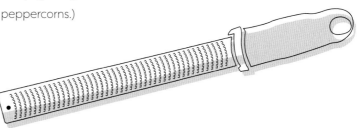

VANILLA BOURBON MARINADE

Courtesy of Sean Brasel • Makes enough for one large roast of pork, veal, or whole chicken

2 cups fresh orange juice

12 grams finely grated lemon zest (about 2 lemons)

15 grams finely grated orange zest (about 2 oranges)

10 grams (1 tablespoon) vanilla extract

1 vanilla bean, seeds scraped from pod, both reserved

2 cups water

45 grams (2 tablespoons) sea salt

½ cup dark agave

½ cup molasses

6 garlic cloves, grated over a Microplane

2 tablespoons fresh thyme

1 cup bourbon

Finished off with freshly grated orange and lemon zest, this always reliable marinade is the perfect mix of acid and sweet for pork, veal, or chicken.

Combine all the ingredients in a large container. Add protein (pork or veal roast or whole chicken). Refrigerate and let marinate for a minimum of 24 hours. Cook protein as desired.

COPPER BOWL

Anne Willan
Founder of Ecole de Cuisine La Varenne
Santa Monica, California

I bought this particular bowl when I lived in France. It came from E.Dehillerin, which has the best equipment for European cooking in the world. This was 1961 and, well, I had been to E.Dehillerin several times. I was a student at the Cordon Bleu in Paris, and everybody talked about E.Dehillerin. I would go and take a look and buy a few little things. I bought at least one knife there; they were all Sabatier knives in those days. But I didn't make an investment in a copper bowl until I actually was catering and earning a bit of money. They're much cheaper in France than they are here—probably half the price. I wanted a size that would allow me to whisk ten egg whites at a time.

Photograph by C. Siri Berting

Mine is a slightly heavier bowl, and it has a very nice big rolled border that you can catch onto. It has a brass ring hanging onto it—quite often when I was teaching, I would catch the attention of the class by holding the bowl up by its ring in one hand and with the other, I would bang it using an oversized balloon whisk. It's a very characteristic sound—there's nothing else like it.

It's crossed the Atlantic many, many times because I used to take it when I was traveling and teaching around the country. Soufflés are my specialty and so it's an essential piece of equipment. It's terribly cumbersome but of course in the old days—that's to say in the '70s and certainly the mid '80s—most cooking schools and cookware stores were not equipped with things like copper bowls. We still use the bowl for teaching—it makes for a good demonstration piece. And it will last forever. In 100 years time, it will be just the same.

> *Quite often when I was teaching, I would catch the attention of the class by holding the bowl up by its ring in one hand and with the other, I would bang it using an oversized balloon whisk.*

When I first came to New York in 1964, I was invited to cook dinner for Craig Claiborne and I made soufflé, as always. It was a shrimp and cheese soufflé and when I brought it out, Craig said, "I knew we would eat well when I heard the sound of the copper bowl."

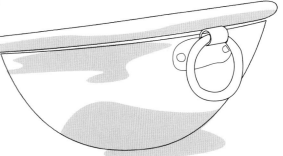

CHOCOLATE SOUFFLÉ

Courtesy of Anne Willan • Serves 4

4 ounces (110 grams) bittersweet chocolate, chopped

½ cup (125 milliliters) heavy cream

3 egg yolks

1½ tablespoons rum or cognac

Melted butter, for the dish

5 egg whites

3 tablespoons (45 grams) granulated sugar

Confectioners' sugar, for sprinkling

Special Equipment: 1-quart (1 liter) soufflé dish or four 1-cup (250 millileters) soufflé dishes

"Chocolate soufflé is so easy," says Willan. "15 minutes prep and 15 minutes to bake. But one reason I love it is that there is always the challenge, the element of risk, like the high jump that you can trip and fall with no halfway of saving face. A relatively high-temperature oven is important in creating a crisp outside and the runny center that forms its own dark chocolate sauce."

For the soufflé mixture, put the chocolate and cream in a saucepan and warm over low heat, stirring often with a wooden spoon until the chocolate is melted and the mixture falls easily from the spoon. Take the pan from the heat and beat in the egg yolks so they cook and thicken the chocolate slightly. Stir in the rum. The soufflé mixture can be prepared to this point 3 to 4 hours ahead, covered and kept in the pan at room temperature.

To finish, heat the oven to 425°F, and set a shelf low down in the oven. Butter the soufflé dish, chill in the freezer until cold, and butter a second time. If using individual dishes, set them on a baking sheet. In a copper bowl (or using a heavy-duty electric mixer), whisk the egg whites until stiff. Gradually add the granulated sugar, whisking to form a light, glossy meringue, about 30 seconds. Warm the chocolate in the pan until just hot to the touch, then remove from the heat and

(continued on next page)

CHOCOLATE SOUFFLÉ *(continued)*

stir in about a quarter of the meringue to lighten it. Add the chocolate mixture to the remaining meringue and fold the mixtures together as lightly as possible. Spoon the mixture into the prepared soufflé dish and smooth the top; the dish should be almost full. Run your thumb around the inside rim of the dish so the soufflé will rise evenly.

Bake the soufflé at once until puffed and almost doubled in volume, 12 to 15 minutes for a large soufflé or 7 to 9 minutes for small ones. If you shake the dish, the soufflé mixture should wobble slightly, showing it is still soft in the center. Meanwhile, line a platter with a napkin so the soufflé dish cannot slide. Take the soufflé from the oven, sprinkle quickly with confectioners' sugar and set the dish on the plate. Serve at once—a soufflé cannot wait. When serving a large soufflé, use 2 large spoons to scoop up both the crisp outside and soft center onto each plate.

CAKE STAND

Rebekah Turshen
Pastry Chef of City House
Nashville, Tennessee

Tom Lazzaro, who owns Nashville's Lazzaroli Pasta, makes all of the pasta for City House—he usually brings us our delivery every week and sometimes he'll bring in some other treats. Tom goes to a lot of kitchen auctions and has a huge collection of stuff. But one day, about three or four years ago, he brought over this cake stand and said it had been in his garage for about ten years. I can't tell if it's actually old or if it just *looks* old, but it's cast iron and painted green, and it has a rubber base. So many of the stands I've used over the years have removable tops, so if you're picking it up, you might lose half the cake, or they slip on the counter. This one is secured together so even though the top turns, it never comes off.

> *Before, I would frost cakes by holding the cake in my right hand and frosting it with my left so that I could get around to all the sides—but that was so dangerous because I'd be balancing this four-inch-high cake on my hands.*

When I started working in bakeries, using a cake stand changed my life. It makes everything so much easier. Before, I would frost cakes by holding the cake in my right hand and frosting it with my left so that I could get around to all the sides—but that was so dangerous because I'd be balancing this four-inch-high cake on my hands. It used to give me "cake wrist." Now, every time I make a cake, I pull this out. It's so functional. You can smooth out the frosting as

you turn it, and I usually lay parchment sheets under the cake to that I can get rid of any of the messier frosted spots before transferring the cake to a plate.

We don't usually keep this stand on display at the restaurant—it mostly lives in a small storage space near the kitchen. And while most of our desserts are pies or cookies, every once in awhile, I make a traditional layer cake. I made chef Tandy Wilson's wedding cake using this stand. And it's perfect for my grandmother's coconut cake with seven-minute frosting. I've made it so many times over the years, including for my own wedding in 2010.

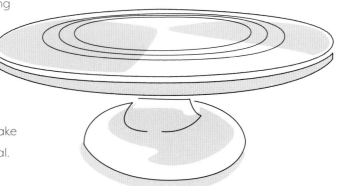

IVA LEE'S COCONUT CAKE *with* SEVEN-MINUTE FROSTING

Courtesy of Rebekah Turshen • Serves 12 to 16

Cake

1⅛ cups unsalted butter

2¼ cups granulated sugar

¾ teaspoon pure vanilla extract

1⅛ cups egg whites

412 grams all-purpose flour (about 3 cups)

1½ teaspoons kosher salt

¾ teaspoon baking powder

¾ teaspoon baking soda

1½ cups whole-fat buttermilk

"My maternal grandmother's name was Iva Lee Haynes," says Turshen. "She always cracked open a whole coconut for this, but I've found it difficult to find a nice fresh one around these parts. Thankfully, plenty of quality, canned coconut milks are available in most grocery stores these days. I like to bake all the layers individually since it's faster to both bake and cool the layers. Plus, they all come out nice and flat, which is perfect for making this nice tall cake. (Alternatively, you can switch it to three pans or two pans, adjust baking time accordingly and slice the layers horizontally.)

"Here's a baker's trick for keeping things neat: Set the first baked layer on the cake stand or cutting board, and lay four strips of parchment paper facing north, south, east, and west just under the edges of the cake. When you're finished assembling and frosting the cake, gently pull out the parchment and voilà!

"I like to serve this at room temperature the first day—but it's delicious straight out of the fridge the following morning for an extra fancy breakfast."

CAKE

Heat the oven to 325°F. Line four 9-inch cake pans with parchment paper and coat with cooking spray.

In a stand mixer, cream together the butter, sugar, and vanilla until light and fluffy. Add the egg whites in three

(continued on next page)

IVA LEE'S COCONUT CAKE *with* SEVEN-MINUTE FROSTING *(continued)*

Frosting

2¼ cups granulated sugar

¼ teaspoon salt

½ teaspoon cream of tartar

1 cup egg whites

⅔ cup cool water

½ teaspoon pure vanilla extract

additions, making sure each is incorporated before adding the next.

In a small bowl, sift together the flour, salt, baking powder, and baking soda. Put the stand mixer speed setting at low. Alternating between the buttermilk and the dry ingredients, add a little bit of each at a time until the mixture is almost smooth. Once everything has been added, turn the mixer speed to high for just a few seconds to aerate the batter.

Evenly divide batter between the pans. Bake for 25 to 30 minutes, until the cakes are firm, golden, and just beginning to separate from the edges of the pans. Let cool in the pans before unmolding.

FROSTING

In a small bowl, combine the sugar, salt, and cream of tartar. Place the egg whites in a medium metal bowl and whisk the dry ingredients in by hand. Add the water and vanilla; whisk to combine.

Place the metal bowl over a saucepan of boiling water and whisk until the mixture reaches a soft peak. Remove from heat and transfer to a stand mixer bowl. Whisk on high until the frosting is no longer warm and holds sharp glossy peaks.

(continued on next page)

IVA LEE'S COCONUT CAKE *with* SEVEN-MINUTE FROSTING *(continued)*

Assembly

1½ cups unsweetened grated coconut

1 16-ounce can unsweetened coconut milk

2 tablespoons sugar syrup

⅛ teaspoon salt

-or-

1 fresh coconut (reserve juice and finely grate meat)

ASSEMBLY

Heat the oven to 325°F.

Place the grated coconut on a sheet pan and toast in the oven for 5 to 10 minutes. Set aside to cool.

Strain or blend the coconut milk to remove lumps, then add the sugar syrup and salt.

Unmold cakes, with the top sides resting on the counter. Peel the parchment off the layers and brush the bottom of each cake with the coconut syrup. Let the cakes sit for several minutes to absorb the liquid before continuing.

Place the first cake layer, syrup-soaked side up, on a cake stand. Place four pieces of parchment under the edges of the cake, north, south, east, and west. Frost the first layer completely, then sprinkle with toasted coconut. Place the second layer on top of first. Repeat with frosting and coconut; continue with remaining layers. Frost the sides and top of the cake. Pat the remaining coconut onto sides of cake with your hands.

Remove the parchment and transfer the cake to a serving platter. Note: You may want to let the cake rest in the refrigerator for an hour or so to set before slicing. Bring the cake out about 30 minutes before serving.

DOUBLE BOILER

Chris Kimball
Founder of America's Test Kitchen
Boston, Massachusetts

I n the '70s, when I started cooking, I shopped at Lamalle Kitchenware, run by Charles Lamalle, in New York, to get my *batterie de cuisine.* It was a wonderful, dumpy place that had a lot of old French cookware, most of it copper. I bought a few things there, but the thing I love the most is the double boiler, which has a porcelain insert in it. People still make them now, but this is the original. And I just find it so interesting because very few recipes call for double boilers anymore, which is curious because there are actually a lot of things you can do with it.

I used to cook on a coal cookstove for a number of years, and using a double boiler is really the equivalent of putting something on the back burner,

> *I've bought a lot of other double boilers over the years—you can also just put a bowl over top of a saucepan—but this one does the best job.*

because it uses a very low, moderate heat. That whole idea, which I think we've lost in many ways, of using this very low heat for long, slow cooking is just something that you don't see much anymore. The Victorians would use these long oblong pans and set jars or little pots of food in them—since water doesn't get over boiling point, they would put that anywhere on the stove and the food would be kept at 212°F. They had a lot of techniques for long, slow cooking and I just think that's anathema to what we do today, unless you're doing sous vide or something.

The one I bought at Lamalle is fairly large, holding about two quarts. It's heavy and just beautiful. I've bought a lot of other double boilers over the years—you can also just put a bowl over top of a saucepan—but this one does the best job. It's been dinged up, of course, and copper turns all sorts of weird colors. I haven't cleaned it in years so it looks like something that's been abandoned. About a year ago, my wife asked if she could use it. Well, she just put the porcelain insert on the heat without the bottom part or the water. That was a close call since it almost cracked. It was a near thing, but I rescued it.

You can do so many things, like melt chocolate or just hold foods, like soups in it, like you would on a back burner. It's a great design—you don't get any better than that.

POTS DE CRÈME

Courtesy of America's Test Kitchen • Serves 8

Pots de Crème

10 ounces bittersweet chocolate, chopped fine (about 1¼ cups; see headnote)

5 large egg yolks

5 tablespoons granulated sugar

¼ teaspoon table salt

1½ cups heavy cream

¾ cup half-and-half

1 tablespoon pure vanilla extract

½ teaspoon instant espresso powder mixed with 1 tablespoon water

"For a pots de crème recipe that would deliver a decadent dessert with a satiny texture and an intense chocolate flavor," writes America's Test Kitchen, *"we moved the dish out of the oven and took an unconventional approach: cooking the custard on the stovetop in a saucepan, then pouring it into ramekins. For the chocolate flavor we wanted, we favored bittersweet chocolate over milk and semisweet chocolate, which we judged to be too mild. At 10 ounces, the chocolate content in our pots de crème was at least 50 percent higher than in any other dessert recipe we've encountered.*

"We prefer pots de crème made with 60 percent cocoa bittersweet chocolate (our favorite brands are Ghirardelli and Callebaut), but 70 percent bittersweet chocolate can also be used. If using a 70 percent bittersweet chocolate (we like Lindt, El Rey, and Valrhona), reduce the amount of chocolate to 8 ounces. A tablespoon of strong brewed coffee may be substituted for the instant espresso and water. Covered tightly with plastic wrap, the pots de crème will keep for up to 3 days in the refrigerator, but the whipped cream must be made just before serving."

POTS DE CRÈME

Place chocolate in medium heatproof bowl; set fine-mesh strainer over bowl and set aside.

(continued on next page)

POTS DE CRÈME *(continued)*

Whipped Cream
½ cup heavy cream (cold)
2 teaspoons granulated sugar
½ teaspoon pure vanilla extract

Garnish (optional)
Cocoa powder, for dusting
Chocolate shavings, for sprinkling

Whisk yolks, sugar, and salt in medium bowl until combined; whisk in heavy cream and half-and-half. Transfer mixture to a medium saucepan. Cook mixture over medium-low heat, stirring constantly and scraping bottom of pot with wooden spoon, until thickened and silky and custard registers 175° to 180°F on instant-read thermometer, 8 to 12 minutes. Do not let custard overcook or simmer.

Immediately pour custard through strainer over chocolate. Let mixture stand to melt chocolate, about 5 minutes. Whisk gently until smooth, then whisk in vanilla and espresso. Divide mixture evenly among eight 5-ounce ramekins. Gently tap ramekins against counter to remove air bubbles.

Cool pots de crème to room temperature, then cover with plastic wrap and refrigerate until chilled, at least 4 hours or up to 72 hours. Before serving, let pots de crème stand at room temperature 20 to 30 minutes.

WHIPPED CREAM

Using a hand mixer or standing mixer fitted with whisk attachment, beat cream, sugar, and vanilla on low speed until bubbles form, about 30 seconds. Increase speed to medium; continue beating until beaters leave trail, about 30 seconds longer. Increase speed to high; continue beating until nearly doubled in volume and whipped cream forms soft peaks, 30 to 45 seconds longer.

Dollop each pot de crème with about 2 tablespoons whipped cream; garnish with cocoa or chocolate shavings, if using. Serve.

TARTE TATIN PAN

Seth Raynor
Chef and Owner of The Pearl and The Boarding House
Nantucket, Massachusetts

I grew up in a family that did a lot of cooking. We lived in a small town in New York where no one ever moved away—there were 20 Raynors within a bike ride of my house. Classic American apple pie was a big part of my childhood. But then, I came out to Nantucket and started working at The Chanticleer, and we had tarte tatin on the lunch menu. I'd never had it growing up or even in culinary school, but once I tried a slice of room-temperature tarte tatin with a little crème fraîche, I thought it was just simple perfection.

About 15 years ago, after we opened The Boarding House, my wife Angela and I were on a trip to Paris, and went into E.Dehillerin, this amazing old-school store with copper everywhere. We saw a tarte tatin pan and

immediately brought it home . . . where it then sat in the closet for years. Eventually, my daughter, Jacq, started getting into baking when she was in her early teens. One day, we were flipping through old cookbooks and found a recipe for tarte tatin. She said, "Dad, I'm going to make that for you." So we pulled out the pan and she started experimenting.

Jacq's 21 now and she's made tarte tatin during the holidays every year since. It's become our father-daughter tradition. We're always debating which type of apple to use or when to add the sugar and butter. She's very much a perfectionist so if it doesn't come out just the way she wants, she gets irritated. Meanwhile, we're just so thankful that she's made this delicious dessert.

You can make tarte tatin in a ten-inch sauté pan, but I prefer using an

> *I'd never had it growing up or even in culinary school, but once I tried a slice of room-temperature tarte tatin with a little crème fraîche, I thought it was just simple perfection.*

actual tarte tatin pan. You really have to cram the apples in—you might think it's going to be eight apples, but it's really going to be ten. When they're lined up side-by-side, the flare of the tarte tatin pan allows them to spread out a bit but still stay in tight so that when you invert the pan, all of the apples stay on the crust.

Now, whenever we have guests over at the holidays, they always comment on Jacq's dessert. It might be just pastry, sugar, butter, and apple—but it looks stunning. For us, it's become an awesome full-circle family experience.

TARTE TATIN

Courtesy of Seth and Jacq Raynor • Serves 8 to 12

200 grams (about 1 cup) plus
4 teaspoons granulated sugar

½ teaspoon plus 1 teaspoon kosher salt

50 grams (about 3½ tablespoons)
plus 140 grams (about 10
tablespoons) unsalted butter,
cubed and kept cold

8 to 10 Granny Smith apples, peeled,
cored, and quartered (this can be
done a day ahead); plus 1 Granny
Smith apple, cored and cut in half
through the center horizontally

1½ cups all-purpose flour

1 egg

3 tablespoons ice water

For serving (optional)
Crème fraîche or vanilla ice cream

"We like to eat tarte tatin at room temperature or just slightly warm," says Raynor, "with a dollop of crème fraîche, which cuts through the caramel really nicely, meaning we can eat more (and that's a good thing!)—but ice cream works just as well."

CARAMEL

Place 200 grams of the sugar in a tarte tatin pan or heavy-gauge 10-inch sauté pan (not nonstick) with a flat bottom. Cook the sugar over medium-low heat until melted and golden brown. Add ½ teaspoon salt and 50 grams of cubed butter. Whisk until the butter is emulsified. Remove from heat.

APPLES

Using the same pan, stand/lean the apple slices against the inner edge of the pan and continue stacking slices around the edge until the pan is fully lined with apples; try to cram one more slice in to keep the layer from falling. Using the same method, create an inner ring. Place half of the horizontally sliced apple in the center to fill the pan. The apples should be standing up snugly and slightly leaning in next to one another.

Place the pan over low heat and cook, rotating the pan about every 45 seconds to avoid creating hot spots. The caramel will start to bubble and the apples will absorb the

(continued on next page)

TARTE TATIN *(continued)*

caramel. Cook for about 10 minutes, until the apples are slightly cooked. Once the caramel is absorbed, place the pan on a rack and let cool.

PASTRY (CAN BE DONE ONE DAY AHEAD)

In a food processor, pulse together the flour, the remaining 4 teaspoons sugar, and 1 teaspoon salt. Add the remaining 10 tablespoons of cold butter cubes and pulse until the butter is broken down to a nice mix of small and large pieces. In a small bowl, beat the egg with the ice water. Add the egg mixture to the food processor and pulse a few times until the dough just starts to come together. (Be careful not to overwork the mixture; if it becomes a ball of dough, try again.)

Empty the loose pastry onto a sheet of parchment paper or plastic wrap and gently form the dough into a disk, gathering up all the loose bits. Do not overwork or allow the dough to become warm. Refrigerate for at least 1 hour or up to 1 day.

TO PREPARE

Heat the oven to 395°F.

Remove the dough from the refrigerator and let sit at room temperature for a few minutes. Dust the dough lightly with flour and, using a rolling pin, carefully flatten and roll out the disk until it's slightly larger than the pan (a little more than 10 inches across). Carefully place the disk over the semicooked apples. Place pan on a rimmed baking sheet and bake for about 35 minutes, rotating halfway through, until the pastry is golden brown.

Remove the pan from the oven and let cool on a rack for at least 20 to 30 minutes. Run a knife or spatula around the inner edge of the pan and then place a large plate upside down over the pastry. Quickly but gently invert the pan and plate. Let the tarte tatin rest a minute, allowing gravity to do its thing. Carefully pry the edge of the pan off of the tarte and remove. Serve slightly warm or at room temperature with crème fraîche or ice cream.

COLLECTION OF
WOODEN SPOONS

Margot McCormack
**Chef / Owner of Margot Café
and Marché Artisan Foods**
Nashville, Tennessee

A s a chef, I have an arsenal of tools to help me
prepare and cook: all manner of knives, French
balloon whisks, an immersion blender, vegetable peeler,
Cuisinart, blender, KitchenAid. But my favorite tool is
the lowly wooden spoon. Not shiny or fancy, nothing
new, no bells and whistles—just simple and sturdy.

The wooden spoon matches my cooking style, which
is more old-fashioned than avant-garde. I gravitate
towards classic recipes prepared in simple ways. Over
the years I have put together a collection of spoons
in all shapes and sizes. Each has a very different feel
in my hand—smooth or rough, a big sturdy grip or a
more fine, delicate one. They are crafted from cherry,
walnut, birch, hickory, beech, and pine. Machine-made

or hand-carved. Big, small, round, flat, short, long.

Each has a specific purpose. Tasting, stirring, scraping. A good wooden spoon is hard to find and so even when the handle gets charred by an open flame or the bowl is cracked or chipped and stained and worn away by time, you hold onto it.

My mother had just such a spoon when I was growing up—a favorite friend to her and so used that it was

> *The wooden spoon matches my cooking style, which is more old-fashioned than avant-garde. I gravitate towards classic recipes prepared in simple ways.*

really nothing but a stick. She let me use it sometimes. A wooden spoon is a safe first tool for a child. There is no danger in stirring except for a little flour on the counter and maybe the floor and perhaps the potential for over-developing gluten. I have eaten a few tough pancakes as a result of enthusiastic stirring by my own four-year-old son, who has vigorously embraced the joy of stirring. My mother's wooden spoon is no longer with us. It had a place of honor in the crock along with the other spoons years after its last go-round in the oatmeal.

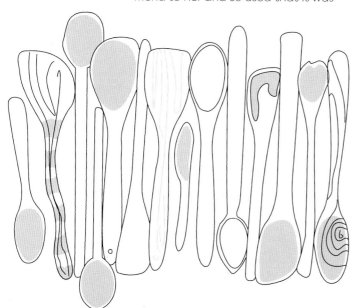

VANILLA ICE CREAM

Courtesy of Margot McCormack • Serves 4

1 quart heavy cream
1 vanilla bean, split
8 egg yolks
1 cup granulated sugar
Special Equipment: Ice cream maker

This classic combination of cream, eggs, and sugar make for a sublime finish to any meal, or a stand alone treat that always delivers.

In a small saucepan, heat the cream and vanilla bean over low heat. Remove and keep warm. In a stainless steel bowl, whisk together the egg yolks and sugar. Pour the cream over the yolks and whisk until combined. Discard the vanilla pod.

Pour the mixture into a large saucepan and cook gently over medium-low heat, stirring with a wooden spoon until the liquid thickens and coats the back the spoon. Strain and chill in an ice bath. Transfer the mixture to an ice cream maker and follow the machine's instructions. Freeze and enjoy.

DEPRESSION-GLASS
JUICER

Jody Adams
Executive Chef of Rialto and TRADE
Boston, Massachusetts

M y grandmother, Helen Henderson Matzke, was one of the hardest-working and most practical people I've known. She was born in 1903 into a family with a private cook and housekeeper. In her late 50s, her family faced financial pressure as her children headed to college, so despite never having held a job outside the home, she climbed behind the wheel of a local school bus carrying children to a neighborhood lower school.

By the time I became aware, her school bus days were long gone, but she embodied the principle of bringing grace and dignity to any work, regardless of your circumstances or job.

My grandmother was a wonderful cook and loved bringing family and friends around her dining room table. She prepared complete meals from scratch three times a day, even at the end of her life when she was living alone.

She started her first book of recipes when she was 11 years old. (I know from whence I came.)

Grocery shopping with her was an adventure, and I paid close attention during visits to Philadelphia. I still remember the little back and forth movements of her thumbs on the steering wheel, and the way the light glinted off the ribs in her nails. She frequented the farmers' market near her home in Germantown, where she brought food fresh from New Jersey farmers. Her favorite vendors knew her by name. In winter, the drive from our home in Providence for holiday gatherings in Pennsylvania seemed endless, but we were always met at the door by the seductive smells of roasting lamb, onions, and potatoes. During the summer,

> *I have more efficient juicers, but none more beautiful, none whose weight feels so right cradled in my palm when I lift it down from the shelf.*

she cooked early in the morning, before the heat, and served us chicken salad with just the right amount of celery and mayonnaise, sliced field tomatoes, and her famous orange cake.

Before she packed up her Philadelphia home and moved into my parents' house, I found this green Depression-glass juicer and measuring cup in her cupboard. She could tell I'd fallen in love with it. I have more efficient juicers, but none more beautiful, none whose weight feels so right cradled in my palm. *She juiced her oranges for the cake with this,* I think. I channel her hands. I've even started to notice ribs in my own thumbnails.

ORANGE CAKE

Courtesy of Jody Adams • Serves 8 to 10

Cake

1 cup unbleached all-purpose flour

1 level teaspoon baking powder

¼ teaspoon salt

⅜ cup milk

3 large eggs, separated and
at room temperature

1 cup granulated sugar

2 teaspoons finely grated orange zest
(about 1 orange)

"This is my grandmother Helen Henderson Matzke's cake recipe," says Adams. *"It's an old-fashioned kind of sponge cake—sort of like an angel food cake. I love it because it's light, easy, bakes quickly, and stands up to the richness of the curd and icing. The icing recipe is one I adapted from the* Joy of Cooking, *our family's favorite cookbook. The curd is my addition to the cake to help balance the sweetness of the icing. I love serving it with unsweetened whipped cream and raspberries."*

CAKE

Heat the oven to 350°F.

Cut 2 rounds of parchment paper and fit them into two 6-inch cake pans. Do not grease the sides of the pan.

Sift the flour into a bowl with the baking powder and salt.

Scald the milk and keep warm.

Beat the egg whites until fluffy. Gradually add half the sugar and continue to beat to soft peaks.

In a large bowl, beat the egg yolks with the orange zest and the remaining sugar until light and fluffy. Fold the whites into the yolks. Sift the flour mixture over the eggs and fold in. Fold in the hot milk. Spoon the mixture into the prepared pans and spread evenly, taking care not to deflate the batter.

Bake until golden on top and a cake tester comes out clean, 25 to 30 minutes. Let cool on wire racks. Once cool, run a knife

(continued on next page)

ORANGE CAKE *(continued)*

Icing

1¼ cups sifted confectioners' sugar

2 tablespoons unsalted butter, at room temperature

1½ teaspoons finely grated orange zest

2 tablespoons orange juice, more as needed

Curd

Finely grated zest and juice of ½ orange

Juice of 2 lemons

½ cup granulated sugar

4 large eggs

6 tablespoons unsalted butter, cut into ½-inch cubes

For Serving (optional)

Unsweetened whipped cream

Fresh raspberries

or spatula around the edges of the cakes and lift them from the pan. Remove and discard the parchment paper.

ICING

Combine all the ingredients in a bowl and beat until smooth. If icing is too thick, add more juice; if icing is too thin, add more sugar.

CURD

Combine the orange zest and juice and the lemon juice in a nonreactive saucepan with the sugar and eggs and beat well. Add the butter and cook over low heat, stirring constantly with a rubber spatula or wooden spoon, until the sugar dissolves and the mixture thickens into a curd. Be sure to keep scraping the bottom of the pan during the few minutes this takes; you don't want the eggs to scramble before the curd forms. Transfer to a small bowl and refrigerate to cool. (Note: You will probably have a little extra curd and icing.)

ASSEMBLING THE CAKE

Put one of the cake layers on a plate. Cover evenly with a thick layer of curd. Top with the second cake layer. Spread a thin layer of icing evenly over the top of the cake. (I don't do the sides because the icing is so sweet.) Chill before slicing. It's best served with unsweetened whipped cream and raspberries.

KITCHENAID
STAND MIXER

Joanne Chang
Pastry chef and Owner of Flour Bakery
Boston, Massachusetts

I didn't plan on becoming a professional pastry chef. My degree from Harvard was in Applied Math and Economics, and after graduation I got a job as a management consultant. I peddled Power Point presentations and Excel spreadsheets by day, but at night I indulged in my true passion and I baked. I baked cookies, cakes, tarts, pies—whatever I could mix sugar and butter into and put in the oven I did.

I worked my way through Maida Heater and Rose Levy Berenbaum and Dorie Greenspan, gleefully making treats for my colleagues and friends. At work I was known as the cookie girl, and there wasn't a pastry I wouldn't make if requested.

It's almost 25 years later and I still have that mixer. The motor is a little choppy and the cord a bit frayed, but it works like a dream, sits on my kitchen counter, and reminds me every day of when I was a 22-year-old wishing I could someday make pastries for a living.

Well, that is, unless it involved whipping up egg whites. In all of the cookbooks I pored over, the recipes that called for making meringues were the only ones out of my reach. Making a great meringue involved a stand mixer, and my meager post-college budget had no room for a piece of equipment that cost almost as much as I was paying in rent. I worked around not having a mixer, whipping by hand whenever possible, making passable pastries with floppy, hand-whipped meringues.

I pined for a KitchenAid mixer (the Cadillac of mixers). I scrimped and saved, and went through the Sunday paper advertisements every week to see if the mixers would go on sale. After about a year, the local Macy's held a blow-out sale of their mixers to make way for a new model, and they were 65 percent off. I coupled that with my recent end-of-year bonus and made my move. I became the proud owner of a KitchenAid.

It was gleaming and shining when I unpacked it and placed it on my tiny kitchen counter in the galley kitchen of my studio apartment. It took up pretty much the whole counter, leaving no room for anything else. But I didn't care. I finally had a mixer!

I made meringue clouds, dacquoise cakes, French macarons, angel food cakes, sponge cakes. A new world of pastry had opened up with the mixer. Having a "professional" piece of baking equipment made me feel like I was taking a step towards maybe, possibly, pursuing this hobby of mine more seriously.

A year later, I left my consulting job and got a job in a 4-star restaurant in Boston. It's almost 25 years later and I still have that mixer. The motor is a little choppy and the cord a bit frayed, but it works like a dream, sits on my kitchen counter, and reminds me every day of when I was a 22-year-old wishing I could someday make pastries for a living.

MERINGUE CLOUDS

Courtesy of Joanne Chang • Makes 8 large clouds

8 egg whites (about 1 cup; 240 grams)

1 cup (200 grams) granulated sugar

1 cup (140 grams) confectioners' sugar

½ teaspoon kosher salt

1 cup sliced and toasted almonds
   or ½ cup finely chopped
   bittersweet chocolate

Adapted from *Flour: Spectacular Recipes from Boston's Flour Bakery + Café* by Joanne Chang (Chronicle Books, October 2010)

Using a workhorse mixer makes quick work of the often fussy task of creating perfect clouds of meringue.

Heat the oven to 175°F. Line a baking sheet with parchment paper.

   In a stand mixer fitted with a whisk attachment or with an electric hand mixer, beat the egg whites on medium speed until soft peaks form, 3 to 4 minutes. The whites will start to froth and turn into bubbles and eventually the yellowy viscous part of the whites will disappear. Keep whipping until you can see the tines of your whisk leaving a slight trail in the whites. Test for soft peak stage by stopping the mixer and removing the whisk from the whites and lifting it up; the whites should peak and then droop.

   With the mixer on medium speed, add the granulated sugar in three increments, mixing for 1 minute between additions. Meanwhile, sift the confectioners' sugar and salt together. Once you've beaten all of the granulated sugar into the egg whites, increase the mixer speed to medium-high and beat for about 30 more seconds. Remove the bowl from the mixer and very slowly and, using a spatula, carefully fold in the confectioners' sugar and salt. Gently fold in the almonds or chocolate, reserving a few tablespoons to garnish the tops of the meringues.

(continued on next page)

MERINGUE CLOUDS *(continued)*

Use a large spoon to scoop out large, baseball-sized, billowing mounds of meringue onto the parchment-lined baking sheet. You should get about 8 meringue clouds. Sprinkle the reserved almonds or chocolate on top of the meringues. Bake for about 3 hours, until the meringues are firm to the touch and you can remove them easily from the baking sheet without having them fall apart. For meringues with a soft, chewy center, remove them from oven at this point and let them cool. For fully crisped meringues, turn off the oven and leave the meringues in it for at least 6 and up to 12 hours. The meringues may be stored in an airtight container at room temperature for up to 5 days.

INDEX

Note: Page numbers in *italics* indicate photographs.

Adams, Jody, *166–70*, 181
appetizers and sides
    Coniglio in "Porchetta,"
        26–28
    Hamachi Tartare with Sweet
        and Sour Tomatoes,
        120–21
    Live Sea Urchin with Fresh
        Grated Wasabi, Lemon,
        and Pickled Mustard
        Seeds, *105–6*
    My Dad's Fried Corn, *48–49*
    Pan Con Tomate, *94–95*
    Pork Skin Risotto, *98–99*
    Roasted Butternut Squash
        & Apples, *64–66*
apples, in Roasted Butternut
    Squash & Apples, *64–66*
apples, in Tarte Tartin, *158–61*
artichokes, in Sustainable Fish
    en Papier, *31–33*

beans and other legumes
    Black Bean Dipping Sauce,
        19
    Diver Scallops with Larded
        Lentils, *40–41*
    Lentil Vinaigrette, 28
    Pole Bean & Medley
        Tomato Salad, *22–23*
beef, in Grilled Beef with Chili
    Vinaigrette & Garlic Chips,
    69–71
Benno, Jonathan, *24–28*, 181
biscuit cutter, *50–51*
biscuits, buttermilk, *52–53*
Black Bean Dipping Sauce, 19
Blue Bay Mussels Provençal,
    44–45
bowl, copper, *140–42*
Brasel, Sean, *136–39*, 181
breads
    Buttermilk Biscuits &
        Crawfish Gravy, *133–35*
    Natalie's Biscuit Recipe,
        102–3
    Pan Con Tomate, *94–95*
    Rebekah's Buttermilk

Biscuits, *52–53*
    Vegetable Corn Bread,
        74–75
Brioza, Stuart, *67–71*, 181
Buttermilk Biscuits & Crawfish
    Gravy, *133–35*

cake stand, *145–46*, *148*
caramel, in Tarte Tartin, *158–61*
carrots, in Moroccan Carrot
    Salad, *112–13*
Cashew or Peanut Curry, *116–17*
Chang, Joanne, *171–76*, 181
Chanin, Natalie, *100–103*, 181
cheese, in Grandma's
    Manicotti, *128–30*
cheese grater, hand-crank,
    126–27
chicken, in Cashew or Peanut
    Curry, *116–17*
chicken, in Great Grandma's
    Chicken Soup, 37
chocolate, in Pots de Crème,
    153–55
Chocolate Soufflé, *143–44*
citrus
    Dutch Baby, *82–83*
    Orange Cake, *168–70*
    Vanilla Bourbon Marinade,
        138–39
cleaver, antique, *62–63*
coconut bench scraper, *114–15*
coconut cake with seven-
    minute frosting, *147–50*
colander, old, *20–21*
Coniglio in "Porchetta," *26–28*
copper bowl, *140–42*
copper jam pot, *54–55*
corn
    My Dad's Fried Corn, *48–49*
    Scallops with Corn Puree
        & Petite Greens Salad,
        86–87
    Vegetable Corn Bread,
        74–75
Crawfish Gravy, 135
cream, whipped, *153–55*
Crushed Tomato Condiment,
    125

Depression-glass juicer, *166–67*

desserts
    Chocolate Soufflé, *143–44*
    Iva Lee's Coconut Cake with
        Seven-Minute Frosting,
        147–50
    Meringue Clouds, *174–76*
    Orange Cake, *168–70*
    Pots de Crème, *153–55*
    Tarte Tartin, *158–61*
    Vanilla Ice Cream, *164–65*
Diver Scallops with Larded
    Lentils, *40–41*
Dutch Baby, *82–83*

eggs, in Chocolate Soufflé,
    143–44
eggs, in Meringue Clouds,
    174–76
Espinosa, Zachary, *84–87*, 181

Fettuccine with Crushed
    Tomato, Blue Crab, and Dill,
    124–25
fish and seafood
    Blue Bay Mussels Provençal,
        44–45
    Buttermilk Biscuits &
        Crawfish Gravy, *133–35*
    Diver Scallops with Larded
        Lentils, *40–41*
    Hamachi Tartare with Sweet
        and Sour Tomatoes,
        120–21
    Live Sea Urchin with Fresh
        Grated Wasabi, Lemon,
        and Pickled Mustard
        Seeds, *105–6*
    Masa Flash-Fried Oysters &
        Pearls, *90–91*
    Scallops with Corn Puree
        & Petite Greens Salad,
        86–87
    Sustainable Fish *en Papier*,
        31–33
fluted Parisian scoop, *118–19*
forks. *See* knives, spoons, and
    forks
fruit
    Dutch Baby, *82–83*
    Roasted Butternut Squash
        & Apples, *64–66*

Tarte Tartin, *158–61*
Fry, Ford, *92–95*, 181

Garlic Chips, *70–71*
Gillespie, Kevin, *96–99*, 181
Grandma's Manicotti, *128–30*
grapefruit, in Dutch Baby,
    82–83
grater, hand-crank cheese,
    126–27
grater, sharkskin wasabi, 104
Great Grandma's Chicken
    Soup, 37
grill, wood-burning indoor,
    92–93
Grilled Beef with Chili
    Vinaigrette & Garlic Chips,
    69–71
Guas, David, *131–35*, 181

Hamachi Tartare with Sweet
    and Sour Tomatoes, *120–21*
Harissa, 113
Hollingsworth, Timothy, *118–21*,
    181
Hopkins, Linton, *107–9*, 181

ice cream, vanilla, *164–65*
Iva Lee's Coconut Cake with
    Seven-Minute Frosting,
    147–50

jam pot, copper, *54–55*
Johnny-Cakes, *108–9*
juicer, Depression-glass,
    166–67

Kimball, Chris, *151–55*, 182
kitchen tools, favorite. *See also*
    knives, spoons, and forks;
    pots and pans
    about: author's selection,
        10–12; insights from, 12–13;
        this book and, 12–13
    baker's spatula, *38–39*
    balloon whisk, *80–81*
    biscuit cutter, *50–51*
    cake stand, *145–46*, *148*
    coconut bench scraper,
        114–15
    colander (old), *20–21*

INDEX *(continued)*

conical steamer, *14–17*
copper bowl, *140–42*
Depression-glass juicer, 166–67
fluted Parisian scoop, 118–19
hand-crank cheese grater, 126–27
Kitchenaid stand mixer, 171–73
metal skewer, 67
microplane, *136–38*
mortar and pestle, 110–11
rolling pin, *100–102*
sharkskin wasabi grater, 104
universal meat grinder, 76–77
wood-burning indoor grill, 92–93
kiwis, in Dutch Baby, *82–83*
knives, spoons, and forks
   antique cleaver, 62–63
   boning knife, 58–59
   knife block, 24–25
   mini meat fork, 122–23
   oyster knife, *88–90*
   plating spoon, 84–85
   silver spoon and cast iron pot, 46–47
   switchblade and pocketknife, 29–30
   wooden spoon(s), 96–97, 131–32, *162–64*
Krasinski, Nicole, 54–57, 182

lentils. *See* beans and other legumes
Levitski, Dale, *80–83*, 182
Live Sea Urchin with Fresh Grated Wasabi, Lemon, and Pickled Mustard Seeds, *105–6*

Masa Flash-Fried Oysters & Pearls, 90–91
mayonnaise, tangy herb, 91
McCormack, Margot, *162–65*, 182
McHugh, Steve, *88–91*, 182
meat grinder, universal, 76–77
Mendenhall, Kyle, *38–41*, 182
Meringue Clouds, *174–76*
metal skewer, 67
microplane, *136–38*
mixer, Kitchenaid stand, 171–73

Moroccan Carrot Salad, *112–13*
mortar and pestle, 110–11
My Dad's Fried Corn, *48–49*

Nana's Ham Salad, *78–79*
Natalie's Biscuit Recipe, *102–3*
Newton, Rob, *46–49*, 182
nuts and seeds
   Cashew or Peanut Curry, *116–17*
   Meringue Clouds, *174–76*
   Peanut Dipping Sauce, 18–19

Orange Cake, *168–70*
Oringer, Ken, *104–6*, 182
oysters, Masa flash fried pearls and, *90–91*

Pan Con Tomate, *94–95*
pancakes (Johnny-Cakes), *108–9*
pasta, Fettuccine with Crushed Tomato, Blue Crab, and Dill, *124–25*
pasta, Grandma's Manicotti, *128–30*
Pig Face Thit Kho, *60–61*
plums, in Strawberry Plum Jam, *56–57*
Pole Bean & Medley Tomato Salad, *22–23*
pork
   Nana's Ham Salad, *78–79*
   Pig Face Thit Kho, *60–61*
   Pork Skin Risotto, *98–99*
pots and pans
   cast iron pan and silver spoon, 46–47
   copper jam pot, 54–55
   copper-bottom Revere Ware pots, 34–35
   double boiler, 151–52
   grandfather's skillet, 107
   Le Creuset Dutch oven, 10–12
   Meme's cast iron skillet, 72–74
   sauté pan, 42–43
   tarte tatin pan, 156–58
Pots de Crème, 153–55

Rabbit Cylinders, *26–28*
Rabbit Mousse, *26–28*

Raynor, Seth, *156–61*, 182
Rebekah's Buttermilk Biscuits, 52–53
rice
   about: sticky rice, 14–16
   Pork Skin Risotto, *98–99*
   Sticky Rice with Peanut Dipping Sauce & Black Bean Dipping Sauce, 18–19
Roasted Butternut Squash & Apples, 64–66
rolling pin, *100–102*
Rushing, Slade, *122–25*, 182

salads
   Moroccan Carrot Salad, *112–13*
   Nana's Ham Salad, *78–79*
   Pole Bean & Medley Tomato Salad, *22–23*
   Scallops with Corn Puree & Petite Greens Salad, *86–87*
Satterfield, Steven, *62–66*, 182
sauces and condiments
   Black Bean Dipping Sauce, 19
   Chili Vinaigrette, 70–71
   Crawfish Gravy, 135
   Crushed Tomato Condiment, 125
   Lentil Vinaigrette, 28
   Peanut Dipping Sauce, 18–19
   Strawberry Plum Jam, 56–57
   Tangy Herb Mayonnaise, 91
   Vanilla Bourbon Marinade, 138–39
Sawyer, Jonathon, *29–33*, 182
scallops. *See* fish and seafood
Scelfo, Michael, *126–30*, 182
Schafer, Sarah, *34–37*, 183
scoop, fluted Parisian, 118–19
scraper, coconut bench, 114–15
seafood. *See* fish and seafood
Sewall, Jeremy, *20–23*, 183
sharkskin wasabi grater, 104
Shaya, Alon, *110–13*, 183
Shepherd, Chris, *58–61*, 183
Sherman, Bruce, *114–17*, 183
side dishes. *See* appetizers and sides
skewer, metal, 67

soup, chicken, 37
spatula, baker's, *38–41*
spoons. *See* knives, spoons, and forks
squash, roasted butternut and apples, 64–66
stand mixer, Kitchenaid, 171–73
steamer, conical, *14–17*
Sticky Rice with Peanut Dipping Sauce & Black Bean Dipping Sauce, 18–19
Strawberry Plum Jam, 56–57
Sustainable Fish *en Papier*, 31–33
Sweet and Sour Tomatoes, 120–21

tapioca, 91
Tarte Tartin, *158–61*
tomatoes
   Crushed Tomato Condiment, 125
   Grandma's Manicotti Sauce, 129
   Pan Con Tomate, 94–95
   Pole Bean & Medley Tomato Salad, *22–23*
   Sweet and Sour Tomatoes, *120–21*
tools. *See* kitchen tools, favorite; knives, spoons, and forks; pots and pans
Turshen, Rebekah, *145–50*, 183

Van Aken, Norman, *76–79*, 183
Vanilla Bourbon Marinade, *138–39*
Vanilla Ice Cream, *164–65*
Vegetable Corn Bread, *74–75*

Whipped Cream, 153–55
whisk, balloon, *80–81*
Wiedmaier, Robert, *42–45*, 183
Willan, Anne, *140–44*, 183
Willis, Virginia, *72–75*, 183
Wilson, Tandy, *50–53*, 183
wood-burning indoor grill, 92–93
wooden spoon(s), 96–97, 131–32, *162–64*

Zimmern, Andrew, *14–19*, 183

RECIPE INDEX

Note: Page numbers in *italics* indicate photographs.

Blue Bay Mussels Provençal | *44-45*

Buttermilk Biscuits & Crawfish Gravy | *133-35*

Cashew or Peanut Curry | *116-17*

Chocolate Soufflé | *143-44*

Coniglio in "Porchetta" | *26-28*

Diver Scallops with Larded Lentils | *40-41*

Dutch Baby | *82-83*

Fettuccine with Crushed Tomato, Blue Crab, and Dill | *124-25*

Grandma's Manicotti | *128-30*

Great Grandma's Chicken Soup | *36-37*

Grilled Beef with Chile Vinaigrette & Garlic Chips | *69-71*

Hamachi Tartare with Sweet and Sour Tomatoes | *120-21*

Iva Lee's Coconut Cake with Seven-Minute Frosting | *147-50*

Johnny-Cakes | *108-109*

Live Sea Urchin with Fresh Grated Wasabi, Lemon & Pickled Mustard Seeds | *105-106*

Masa Flash-Fried Oysters & Pearls | *90-91*

Meringue Clouds | *174-176*

Moroccan Carrot Salad | *112-113*

My Dad's Fried Corn | *48-49*

Nana's Ham Salad | *78-79*

Natalie's Biscuit | *102-103*

Orange Cake | *168-170*

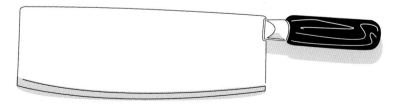

RECIPE INDEX *(continued)*

Pan Con Tomate | *94-95*

Pig Face Thit Kho | *60-61*

Pole Bean & Medley Tomato Salad | *22-23*

Pork Skin Risotto | *98-99*

Pots de Crème | *153-155*

Rebekah's Buttermilk Biscuits | *52-53*

Roasted Butternut Squash & Apples | *64-66*

Scallops with Corn Puree & Petite Greens Salad | *86-87*

Sticky Rice with Peanut Dipping Sauce & Black Bean Dipping Sauce | *18-19*

Strawberry Plum Jam | *56-57*

Sustainable Fish *en Papier* | *31-33*

Tarte Tartin | *158-161*

Vanilla Bourbon Marinade | *138-139*

Vanilla Ice Cream | *164-65*

Vegetable Corn Bread | *74-75*

CONTRIBUTORS

Adams, Jody
Rialto, Trade (Boston, MA)

Benno, Jonathan
Lincoln Ristorante (New York, NY)

Brasel, Sean
Meat Market (Miami, FL)

Brioza, Stuart
State Bird Provisions, The Progress (San Francisco, CA)

Chang, Joanne
Flour Bakery (Boston, MA)

Chanin, Natalie
Alabama Chanin (Florence, AL)

Espinosa, Zachary
Harbor House (Milwaukee, WI)

Fry, Ford
The Optimist, King + Duke, Superica, Marcel, El Felix, St. Cecilia, No 246, JCT Kitchen (Atlanta, GA)

Gillespie, Kevin
Gunshow, Revival (Atlanta, GA)

Guas, David
Bayou Bakery Coffee Bar & Eatery; American Grilled (Arlington, VA)

Hollingsworth, Timothy
Otium L.A. (Los Angeles, CA)

Hopkins, Linton
Restaurant Eugene, Holeman and Finch Public House, Linton's in the Garden, H&F Burger, Hop's Chicken (Atlanta, GA)

CONTRIBUTORS *(continued)*

Kimball, Chris
Founder of America's Test Kitchen (Boston, MA)

Krasinski, Nicole
State Bird Provisions, The Progress (San Francisco, CA)

Levitski, Dale
Sinema, The Hook (Nashville, TN)

McCormack, Margot
Margot Café, Marché Artisan Foods (Nashville, TN)

McHugh, Steve
Cured (San Antonio, TX)

Mendenhall, Kyle
The Kitchen Restaurants (Boulder, CO)

Newton, Rob
Wilma Jean, Nightingale 9 (Brooklyn, NY)

Oringer, Ken
Clio, Uni, Toro, Coppa, Earth (Boston, MA)

Raynor, Seth
The Pearl, The Boarding House (Nantucket, MA)

Rushing, Slade
Brennan's Restaurant (New Orleans, LA)

Satterfield, Steven
Miller Union (Atlanta, GA)

Sawyer, Jonathon
The Greenhouse Tavern, Trentina, Tavern Vinegar Company (Cleveland, OH)

Scelfo, Michael
Alden & Harlow (Cambridge, MA)

Schafer, Sarah
Irving Street Kitchen (Portland, OR)

Sewall, Jeremy
Lineage, Island Creek Oyster Bar, Row 34, Eastern Standard Kitchen & Drinks (Boston, MA)

Shaya, Alon
Shaya, Domenica, Pizza Domenica (New Orleans, LA)

Shepherd, Chris
Underbelly (Houston, TX)

Sherman, Bruce
North Pond (Chicago, IL)

Turshen, Rebekah
City House (Nashville, TN)

Van Aken, Norman
Norman's Restaurant (Orlando, FL)

Wiedmaier, Robert
Marcel's (Washington D.C.)

Willan, Anne
Ecole de Cuisine La Varenne (Santa Monica, CA)

Willis, Virginia
Cookbook author (Atlanta, GA)

Wilson, Tandy
City House (Nashville, TN)

Zimmern, Andrew
Bizarre Foods with Andrew Zimmern (Minneapolis, MN)

MORE GREAT BOOKS *from*
SPRING HOUSE PRESS

The Cocktail Chronicles
ISBN: 978-1-940611-17-4
List Price: $24.95 | 200 Pages

**Secrets from the
La Varenne Kitchen**
ISBN: 978-1-940611-15-0
List Price: $17.95 | 136 Pages

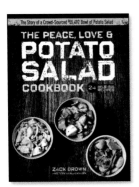

**The Peace, Love &
Potato Salad Cookbook**
ISBN: 978-1-940611-38-9
List Price: $16.95 | 80 Pages

The Natural Beauty Solution
ISBN: 978-1-940611-18-1
List Price: $19.95 | 128 Pages

The Hot Chicken Cookbook
ISBN: 978-1-940611-19-8
List Price: $19.95 | 128 Pages

SPRING HOUSE PRESS

Look for these Spring House Press titles at your favorite bookstore, specialty retailer, or visit *www.springhousepress.com*.
For more information about Spring House Press, call 717-208-3739 or email us at *info@springhousepress.com*.